ENDORSEMENTS

As a believer, I feel that we need to know the power of the Holy Spirit. From the minute I started reading the book, my eyes opened to how much more we can achieve and do through the unction of the Holy Spirit. The book is very clear and easy to understand. The scriptures support the points in the book very well. This book finally helped me to understand that any believer can prophesy and that prophesying is as easy as speaking in tongues. I would recommend this book to pastors so that they can empower their congregants to prophesy, and to new believers so that they can fully experience the power of the Holy Spirit.

---------*Sister Rose, a Young Believer in Christ*

The Prophetic Revolution is a timely message from God to the end-time Church to flow in revival and harvest. It is a key tool for those who are in leadership and for believers to understand the importance of the prophetic voice. I highly recommend this book and pray that it will open the eyes of many people, and be used as a channel to pave the way for communicating God's prophetic message to the Church and the world.

---------*Bishop Sam Kumar, India Center for Revival. Dubbed the "John the Baptist of India" by Charisma Magazine.*

The timing of Bishop Reid's book, **The Prophetic Revolution** is a God-sent by the Holy Spirit. Over the last one hundred years, the devil has worked hard to silence the voice of the prophetic and prophecy. Now is the time in these last days for the prophets to awaken and arise and show the world, God is real, and Jesus is returning soon. An army needs to awaken and warn the world that judgment is coming. Praise God for the hand of the Holy Spirit for giving us this timely great awakening with this book.

---------*Pastor David White, Full-Time Missionary to Brazil and Itinerate Preacher Worldwide.*

For any message to be delivered it must first be given. God's instruction is tantamount and clear when he told Ezekiel to prophesy to the valley of dry bones (Ezekiel 37). There are no reservations concerning God's command. Therefore, I am feeling excited about this book as a guideline, **The Prophetic Revolution**. Get ready for the fire of God to unleash in a greater proportion as there will be another generation who will learn to hear the voice of God and then prophesy accordingly.

---------Bishop Dr. Gary Howe, Host of The Gospel Light Radio Broadcast, United Kingdom. Regional Overseer over Multiple Churches in Europe.

This is amazing, God-led writing, a major blessing to the body of Christ, which time has come.

---------Bishop Dr. K. D. Collins, Chief Presiding Bishop of Harvest Army Church International

A treasure for these end times, **The Prophetic Revolution** is a timely resource for every Christian, church leader and the body of Christ collectively. Fostering the prophetic, this gift opens the eyes of believers to God's prophetic call in their lives. As a useful tool, **The Prophetic Revolution** guides church leaders in empowering and leading their churches into the prophetic. This asset will no doubt mobilize the body of Christ into manifestations of the prophetic plunging the church into a prophetic revolution!

---------Reverend S. Mckoy, Harvest Army Church International

The Prophetic Revolution

OMAUDI D. REID

FOREWORD BY BISHOP DR. K. D. COLLINS

Harvesters Online Publishing

The Prophetic Revolution

By Omaudi D. Reid

Copyright © 2019 by Harvesters Online Publishing

www.harvestersonline.com

New York

All rights reserved. No part of this book may be reproduced or transmitted in any form or by any means without written permission from the publisher.

Unless otherwise noted, all Bible quotations are from the King James Version. The author added an emphasis to portions of some Scripture verses; the added emphasis are the bolded portions of the Bible verse.

ISBN 978-1-7334859-0-6

Printed in USA

DEDICATION AND ACKNOWLEDGEMENTS

In 1993, my mother took my sister and I to the Harvest Army Church International at the time located in Yonkers, New York. The pastor was Bishop Keith Collins. At the time, I thought his preaching was unique. It was through his ministry that God began to work in my life. Being a woman of prophetic insight, my mother believed when the pastor told her that I would become a member of the church, and later that I was called to the ministry. I am forever grateful to the Lord for using my mother to bring me to a place that continues to have an eternal impact on my life.

Hence, this book would not have been possible without the leadership of Bishop Dr. K. D. Collins, now the Chief Presiding Bishop of the Harvest Army Church International. God has used him as a vessel to trigger world revival. The Harvest Army Church International has been used by God to sponsor Worldwide Vision Day, a call for all churches and believers worldwide to unite on the first Saturday of each quarter (every three months) to preach the gospel of Jesus Christ on the streets and marketplaces of their city – one voice, one hour, one accord.

Furthermore, the prophetic revolution is evident in the Harvest Army Church body as thousands of prophecies are released from the leaders and members of the church that consistently come to pass. The members of the church can be seen weekly preaching the gospel of Jesus Christ in their community and prophesying the return of Jesus Christ. I dedicate this book to the Harvest Army Church International church body, and for the vision for world revival.

Thanks to my wife, who I came to know by revelation. She has been a constant encouragement to complete this book. Evidence of her support is in the pages of the book since she shared her own insights and testimony. She supports my writing not only out of love for me, but also because God revealed to her over twelve years ago that writing books should be a part of our ministry. I thank her for her faithfulness in supporting my life and ministry.

Table of Contents

FOREWORD VII

1. THE PROPHETIC REVOLUTION – WHAT AND WHY? 1
2. THE BIBLICAL PROGRESSION TOWARDS PROPHETIC EXPLOSION 15
3. CLARIFYING PROPHETIC TERMS 25
4. PROPHETIC COMMODITY 33
5. THE GREAT VALUE OF PROPHECY 41
6. PROPHETIC REVELATION FOR LIFE DECISIONS 53
7. THE GIFT OF PROPHECY 79
8. PROPHETIC REVELATION 93
9. HOW TO RECEIVE THE GIFT OF PROPHECY 113
10. THE MINISTRY OFFICE OF PROPHET 123
11. BECOMING A PROPHETIC CHURCH 139
12. GUARDING AGAINST FALSE PROPHECY 161
13. THE EYEWITNESSES 171
14. PROPHETIC LITERACY 179
15. THE LAST STANDOFF 207

APPENDIX 215

   DID THE PROPHETIC GIFT CEASE? A BIBLICAL RESPONSE TO THE OBJECTION OF CESSATIONISM 215

FOREWORD

This book "A Prophetic Revolution" is an amazing manuscript which time has come, at a juncture in the history of mankind when suicide among clergymen have rocked the church. Most believers in Christ are shocked. This because of a dearth in prophetic knowledge as the Scripture prophesied would happen in the last days (Amos 8:11-12).

Bishop Omaudi Reid is uniquely qualified to pen this book because of his leadership in a church body which has prophesied much of the global events in the past 20 years. He is the Chairman of "Worldwide Vision Day" a movement that mobilizes the body of Christ to go on the highways and edges on the same day every first Saturday of every quarter, since July 4, 2014. He is also well studied in the fields of theology and education.

The book identifies the inexcusable call to preach the gospel and to employ the prophetic gifts to bring maximum results. It is scholastic but very easy to read as he uses many gripping examples and testimonies to bear out the categorical layout.

Every chapter is intriguing, but my favorite is "The Last Standoff". This is because it entails daring prophecies with striking details of what is ahead of us. When you have finished reading this book, you will not be shocked with abnormalities that inundate the world and even many churches today. You will appreciate the value of prophecy, receive the gifts, and your church will become a more prophetic one. Enjoy it.

1

THE PROPHETIC REVOLUTION – WHAT AND WHY?

HEARING THE DIVINE alarm, an army of *prophets* arises around the world. Like commandos positioned in every continent, they have a fiery weapon in their mouth that burns the hearts of men. They are coming out of the caves where they were hiding and awakening from the slumber of the night. With the fear of God consuming their hearts, the army no longer runs from the ridicules of the world, nor the objections of the lukewarm church.

The enemies of God find that they are not a standard set of soldiers. Unknown and unlisted, their clothing seems pedestrian. Although moving like the wind, their feet step with an ambassador's authority. Carrying a message that cuts the hearts of some, yet remains irresistible to others. Troubling the idolatrous, stinging the satanists, yet drawing the hungry, these things are the effects of their presence and words. The sudden and bold revealing of this prophetic army even stuns the prime ministers and presidents. It's the rise - of a prophetic revolution.

Why a Prophetic Revolution?

The church worldwide is under siege in many aspects, including persecution, threatening laws, homosexual activism, and false doctrines. There is a concerted global effort to put the church in a cave – to make the practice of Christianity a private matter, but limited or banned in the public square. Persecution is on the rise throughout Africa and the Middle East. At times, entire villages of Christians are being slaughtered by Islamic terrorists even in places like Nigeria and Kenya where much of the population are Christians[i]. China's bizarre persecution of the church now includes removing crosses from church buildings, demanding the removal of certain parts of the ten commandments, monitoring online religious activity, along with increasing the imprisonment of many believers. Even the government-sanctioned churches of China are experiencing persecution[ii]. Beyond the Middle Eastern countries with laws restricting religious freedom, Russia, Nepal, Sri Lanka, Myanmar, Bhutan, parts of India, and parts of Pakistan have enacted anti-evangelism laws[iii]. Most of Europe has limited the freedom to evangelize through vague hate speech laws[iv]. In the United States, some politicians argue that religious practice should be private. A few American politicians even publicly suggest that people of faith should change their beliefs to fit the culture.

Many church leaders respond to these threats through political activism, debates, lobbying, social engagement, media outreach, education, and similar activities. While these actions are acceptable, they will not sufficiently counter the concerted effort to corner the church. However, the solution has already been prophesied in the Word of God. When a nation, a people, or the world thump their fists against God and his people, God responds supernaturally, beginning with the utterance of His word. God raises up and sends prophets: Noah to build an ark, Moses to speak to Pharaoh, Samuel to enlighten a nation, Elijah to call the nation back to God. God's answer to the threats against the church is a manifestation of the Spirit of Prophecy through gospel-truth believers. The prophetic revolution is a trumpet in the mouth of the church, the pulpit and pew, preaching the gospel with prophetic manifestations and power.

The Revolution in Action

Preaching one Sunday morning, through the Spirit I spontaneously said: *"Even while I am speaking right now, don't be too disengaged. Don't be distracted. Don't just be a spectator. Maybe God has a word in you right now that you need to speak. For this is a place of Revelation"*. Those were the words I spoke in my church in February of 2018. A few minutes later, I was unable to finish the sermon, as several of the members began prophesying one after the other as the Spirit gave them utterance. The Lord has been laying on my spirit that the gift of prophecy should be a common operation in the church. The Spirit of God mightily moved in the church as the members prophesied. The Lord was demonstrating His will for the manifestation of the gift of prophecy among his people.

Beyond my local church, God's desire for the whole earth to be filled with the knowledge of the glory of God is bringing about an explosive manifestation of the prophetic gift around the world. God has been expressing His will in the earth through prophetic utterances and revelations since ancient times.

But today more than ever, many are operating in the gift of prophecy all over the world. This is happening in several churches and ministries around the globe. However, I am intimately aware of the prophetic mantle that has been released in my church body, a ministry that is triggering revival worldwide. There are at least five ways God is using common men and women in this prophetic movement:

Gospel Preaching

Revelation 19:10 ...the testimony of Jesus is the Spirit of Prophecy

1 Peter 1:10-11 Of which salvation **the prophets** *have inquired and searched diligently, who* **prophesied** *of the grace that should come unto you: Searching what, or what manner of time the* **Spirit of Christ** *which was in them did signify, when it* **testified beforehand** *the sufferings of Christ, and the glory that should follow.*

The gospel of Jesus Christ is prophetic because it is the primary fulfillment of the prophecies, types, and shadows of the Old Testament. Secondly, the gospel provides the bridge for the fulfillment of the biblical prophecies of the future.

The gospel of Jesus Christ is that Jesus Christ died, was buried and on the third day rose again. It includes that Christ will return to judge the world and establish His kingdom on the earth.

When believers preach the gospel of Jesus Christ, they are operating in the Spirit of Prophecy. They are testifying of Christ's redemption, which is a fulfillment of Old Testament prophecies; they prophesy in accordance with Scripture of His second return to judge humankind.

THE PROPHETIC REVOLUTION – WHAT AND WHY?

Mark 1:1-4 The beginning of the gospel of Jesus Christ, the Son of God; As it is written in the prophets, Behold, I send my messenger before thy face, which shall prepare thy way before thee. The voice of one crying in the wilderness, Prepare ye the way of the Lord, make his paths straight. John did baptize in the wilderness, and preach the baptism of repentance for the remission of sins.

Isaiah 40:9-10 O Zion, that bringest good tidings, get thee up into the high mountain; O Jerusalem, that bringest good tidings, lift up thy voice with strength; lift it up, be not afraid; say unto the cities of Judah, Behold your God! Behold, the Lord GOD will come with strong hand, and his arm shall rule for him: behold, his reward is with him, and his work before him.

Just as John the Baptist was a voice in the wilderness preparing the way of the Lord, even so believers today are preaching the gospel in preparation of Christ's second coming. Like Zion, the church is being called to raise our voices in declaring that the Lord is coming.

2 Peter 1:19-21 We have also a more sure word of prophecy; whereunto ye do well that ye take heed, as unto a light that shineth in a dark place, until the day dawn, and the day star arise in your hearts. Knowing this first, that no prophecy of the scripture is of any private interpretation. For the prophecy came not in old time by the will of man: but holy men of God spake as they were moved by the Holy Ghost.

If believers preach the gospel according to the Scriptures, they are reporting the testimony given by the Holy Spirit. Believers can preach the gospel of Jesus by quoting the Bible verses on Christ's redemptive work since the Holy Spirit fully inspires the Scriptures.

There is a sharp uptick in the mobilization of believers to preach the gospel throughout the body of Christ. A growing movement, Worldwide Vision Day, is when believers unite worldwide in one day to preach the gospel, on the first Saturday of every quarter (www.worldwidevisionday.org). Global Outreach Day, which calls on believers to evangelize on the same day, occurs once a year on the last Saturday in May (GlobalOutreachDay.com). The Send is a movement that is mobilizing believers in the United States to win the world for Christ (TheSend.org). Moreover, now, thousands of churches and parachurch organizations worldwide mobilize every believer to evangelize. These are some of the things God is doing to stir His people to preach the gospel.

> CHRISTIANS WHO DECLARE THE GOSPEL HAVE GREATER PROPHETIC INSIGHT.

Christians who declare the gospel have greater prophetic insight because *the testimony of Jesus is the Spirit of Prophecy* (Revelation 19:10). Furthermore, Daniel 12:3 tells of the wise who *turn many to righteousness*, along with Daniel 11:33 that declares that they that understand will *instruct many*. The Harvest Army World Revival Movement with the vision of "an army of harvesters for world revival" is impacting multiple churches and denominations by empowering every believer to preach the gospel (www.harvestarmy.org). Through the movement, young and old across genders and cultures preach the gospel regularly. Subsequently, a prophetic mantle often operates throughout the movement. This is evidence that the preaching of the gospel brings believers into the prophetic unction.

Prophetic Utterances

Another way the prophetic revolution is unveiling is in prophetic utterances. The believer speaks a message as the Spirit of God gives it. Just as believers speak in tongues as the Spirit gives the utterance, the Holy Spirit also provides the utterance for believers to declare a message in the common language of the hearers. This is not merely preaching a sermon, but a supernaturally given utterance. This often happens during local church services, but also occurs in any arena as the Spirit moves. It is often an exhortation, warning, or a comforting word that is given through the believer to the hearers. It does not have to include a specific revelation of the future or something unknown but often is an admonition.

The Scriptures speak of this below:

It's a spiritual gift

1 Corinthians 12:10 ..**to another prophecy**

Speaks for edification, exhortation, and comfort

1 Corinthians 14:3 But he that prophesieth speaketh unto men to edification, and exhortation, and comfort.

It's to be desired by all believers

1 Corinthians 14:1 Follow after charity, and desire spiritual gifts, but rather that ye may prophesy.

All can prophesy

1 Corinthians 14:5 I would that ye all spake with tongues, but rather that ye prophesied.

1 Corinthians 14:24 But if all prophesy, and there come in one that believeth not, or one unlearned, he is convinced of all, he is judged of all:

Prophetic Revelation

The prophetic revolution comes with an explosion of revelatory gifts. Revelations of the future, present, or past are being released in utterance, or writing; God is confirming the revelations with constant fulfillments. The Lord may give the revelation through a dream, vision, or simply the voice of the Holy Spirit.

A growing believer, who at the time was only two years in the Christian faith, received a revelation of an underwater volcano erupting. The revelation was tested and then published on the Harvest Army Church International website on March 6, 2013. The fulfillment of this was posted on June 26, 2013, where an underwater volcano was reported from India. Later other developments were published on September 6, 2013 (Youtube.com/HarvestArmy). The sister, a new Christian attending the church for only two years, gave the revelation. She is not a part of the clergy, nor does she or others claim that she is a prophet; rather, she is a devoted church worker who hears from God. There are many similar examples.

A prophetic revelation can be given through a prophetic utterance. In other words, a revelation may be released as a believer is given the message to speak. This took place with my wife in her early Christian years. The following is an account of the event in the words of my wife, Pastor Guerline Reid:

> *The Holy Spirit was heavy within the service, and people were crying out to God for his anointing. Being only a young convert, the preacher called me to come to the altar. I looked both ways as if to say "he must be calling on someone else and he looked and pointed at me and asked me to come. I did not understand it, but I went to the altar. As the preacher opened his mouth and said the glory of the Lord is upon this one and laid his hands upon me, I saw fire coming from his hand and inside of me. I jumped and cried out glory repeatedly. When I opened my eyes, I was at a different location of the church, and I was shaking with the power of God. Immediately I heard a voice speaking to me, and I knew it was the Lord. The voice said go to your aunt's house; there is a spirit of death in her house, and I want you to go pray in her house. I immediately told this to two others who accompanied me to her house. As we entered the house, I started crying and wailing and warning her of what the Lord said would come if she did not set her house in order. The Lord revealed a plan that her boyfriend planned to destroy her through the spirit of witchcraft. As I prophesied to her, the Spirit of the Lord filled the room, and the other two young ladies started to speak in tongues as I continued to prophesy under the power of God. I spoke in tongues for the very first time'. That night the Lord continued to be upon me heavily. The Lord continued to teach me through his words, and as I prayed, the Lord would reveal the hidden secrets of others.*

In another example, a prophetess spoke a revelation under the unction of the Holy Spirit on November 7, 2018, at approximately 10 pm at a church in New York City. Below is the prophecy:

> *You are my chosen vessel. Remain in Zion and watch, watch, watch, for there is a wave of EXCESS EVIL that is about to sweep the earth. Watch, watch, watch, I've seen the wave. I've seen the wave of EVIL about to hit the earth. Watch, children watch. Watch, there is about to be a SLAUGHTER. Watch, watch for the children. Watch, watch for your children, watch for your children, Watch, watch.*

The next day, November 8, 2018 a slaughter took place in California, United States. This was a prophetic revelation that was released in an utterance.

Prophecy During Evangelism

God is giving believers who preach and share Christ in their local streets and marketplaces, prophetic revelations of unbelievers to aid in their witness. The revelation may reveal bondages, or issues in the life of the unbeliever, that when spoken, brings conviction in the heart of the sinner.

For example, I know a woman who evangelizes effectively in her neighborhood and on the streets. She has no ministerial training and never attended college; however, she shares the gospel personally with others better than many seminary-trained ministers. What's her secret? God reveals to her issues in the life of unbelievers. So, as she shares how Christ can make a difference in the problems of their lives, they feel like she understands them, and they open their hearts to her words.

While sharing the gospel with a couple in the streets of New Jersey, the Holy Spirit revealed to her that they were homeless, unmarried, and using drugs. She began telling them about their situation, and they began to cry. The couple accepted her prayers. Then, they confessed Jesus Christ as their Savior. Another time, she was street preaching in Queens, New York. There were a group of men in the vicinity, and the Lord began showing her their activities. Without having any observable evidence, she saw by the Spirit that they were gangsters. She began preaching for them to repent of their lifestyle. Some loudly resisted saying they would not change. However, one responded in repentance, and another sought for prayer.

We see this in Christ's dialogue with the woman at the well. The Samaritan woman at the well first thought Jesus was a prophet as He exposed her sins (John 4:19). While speaking to the Samaritan woman, Jesus revealed that she had five husbands (John 4:16-19). Due to this, her heart opened to Christ's words. Shortly after, she realized that Jesus was the Christ, and told the people of her community of a man that exposed all she ever did.

1 Corinthians 14:24-25 But if all prophesy, and there come in one that believeth not, or one unlearned, he is convinced of all, he is judged of all: And thus are the secrets of his heart made manifest; and so falling down on his face he will worship God, and report that God is in you of a truth.

The above Scripture verses demonstrate the convicting power of prophecy. Through prophetic utterance and revelation, unbelievers can be convicted of the sins in their hearts and turn to God. The prophetic unction gives humankind an encounter with God. Furthermore, in general, unbelievers can understand prophecies and fulfillments even more quickly than systematic theology.

Prophetic Revelation for Life Decisions

There are many examples of prophetic revelation for personal guidance. Without a doubt, God speaks to his people on an individual basis. Often God will give the believer a sense of peace, nudging guidance, or a prompting in a particular direction. But God also directs his people through dreams, visions, word of knowledge, and other revelations. In this time, when God is pouring out his Spirit, these manifestations will become even more prevalent. God is giving prophetic revelations to guide his people in decisions for marriage, ministry, career, businesses, and more.

The Prophetic Revolution is Unfolding

This explosion of prophetic gifting manifests itself among people of all ages. Beyond the clergy, laymen, boys and girls are operating in the gift of prophecy and receiving prophetic revelation. I have seen pre-teens, teenagers, and adults release prophetic utterances under the power of the Spirit of God. Hundreds of prophetic revelations have been given by everyday members of the church that has been fulfilled. Also, I have personally experienced regular church members give prophetic revelations that personally impacted my life. For example, in 2014, a new member of the church I pastored had a revelation seeing my car in a near collision with another vehicle; he told me to be careful while driving. A few days later, while driving on the highway, I notice the car in front seemed to be out of control. I had slowed my driving taking heed to the prophetic revelation that was given. I had the collision, but my family and I were completely safe. Another time, while praying concerning the church finances and telling God how much money the church needed, the Holy Spirit led me to request a higher amount. I asked for the amount that the Holy Spirit placed in my heart. Afterward, I got up from my knees and immediately got a call from one of the ladies in my church. She told me her dream, how our executive pastor asked a specific amount for the church offering; the same amount of money given by the Holy Spirit. Beyond this, on the Harvest Army World Revival Movement's YouTube channel (Youtube.com/harvestarmy), are many fulfilled prophetic revelations that were spoken by laymen.

However, this phenomenon is not limited to members of my church. Instead, God is pouring His Spirit on the current generation bringing about a prophetic revolution in our time.

Joel 2:28 And it shall come to pass afterward, that I will pour out my spirit upon all flesh; and your sons and your daughters shall prophesy, your old men shall dream dreams, your young men shall see visions:

This Prophetic Revolution is:

For All People - The Spirit of Prophecy is coming upon people from all over the world from every culture. "All Flesh" means all people groups from every culture, language, and nation. This is already happening as believers from different cultures are prophesying by the power of God.

For Male and Female - The Spirit of Prophecy is poured upon males and females alike. Women are prophesying as well as men.

To emphasize that this is for both male and female, God repeats it in verse 29 of Joel when he says, and on your "servants" and "handmaids" he will pour out his Spirit. Servants are male servants; handmaids are female servants. God wanted to ensure us that the prophetic outpouring will take place on both biological sexes. Wise church leaders will release women to walk in the Spirit of Prophecy.

For Young and Old - The outpouring is taking place across multiple generations - children, young, middle-aged, and old. Both young and old will be receiving prophetic revelation in this time. We are witnessing teenagers, young adults, and even small children uttering prophetically and receiving prophetic revelation. Wise church leaders will cultivate even young children to prophesy under the power of God.

For Rich and Poor - The outpouring is taking place across all social classes. This is not limited to the wealthy, nor is it just among the less wealthy, but across all communities with people from multiple career backgrounds, the spirit of prophecy is being outpoured.

This prophetic revolution is the solution to the concerted effort around the world to corner the church – the pulpit and pew, arising in preaching the gospel with prophetic manifestation and power. When believers unite locally, nationwide, regionally, and worldwide, preaching the gospel with the Spirit of Prophecy flowing through them in supernatural utterances, prophetic insight, and revelations, the church will not be silenced.

2

THE BIBLICAL PROGRESSION TOWARDS PROPHETIC EXPLOSION

THE BIBLE IS a prophetic book. As such, it can be said that God is the first Prophet. God's word is always true because His word creates or brings things into action. He gave a prophecy in the book of Genesis of the coming Messiah. Then God began to reveal the things to come to men, and those men would prophesy to others. He revealed the coming judgment to Noah, who uttered the warning to the people. He revealed his plans for Israel to Abraham. The patriarchs, Abraham, Isaac and Jacob all prophesied, and even Joseph prophesied concerning Israel's future. Then we have Moses, and other spoken prophets. By the time of the Kings in Israel there were notable prophets, spoken prophets, and lay prophets. A school of prophets was even established. There were prophets from all walks of life.

The All-Knowing Prophet

God gave the first redemptive prophecy written in Scripture in Genesis 3:15. God knows all and reveals things as He pleases.

Obviously, God stands apart and above all other prophets since He performs that which He speaks. Jesus Christ is the All-Knowing Prophet; the Word in the flesh; the full expression of the glory of God. In prophesying of the All-Knowing Prophet, Moses said this: *"The Lord thy God will raise up unto thee a Prophet from the midst of thee, of thy brethren, like unto me, unto him ye shall hearken"* (Deuteronomy 18:15; Acts 3:22-24; Acts 7:37-40). God has been revealing himself through His Son (Acts 7:37-38). He has also been speaking through the prophets of old about the new covenant in Christ. The fulfillment of prophecy reveals that God truly is real.

Isaiah 46:10 Declaring the end from the beginning, and from ancient times the things that are not yet done, saying, My counsel shall stand, and I will do all my pleasure:

Isaiah 48:3 I have declared the former things from the beginning; and they went forth out of my mouth, and I shewed them; I did them suddenly, and they came to pass.

Isaiah 45:21 Tell ye, and bring them near; yea, let them take counsel together: who hath declared this from ancient time? who hath told it from that time? **have not I the LORD?** *and there is no God else beside me; a just God and a Saviour; there is none beside me.*

Isaiah 42:9 Behold, the former things are come to pass, and new things do I declare: before they spring forth I tell you of them.

Prophecy sets God apart among the false idols, and confirms Christ's deity. The All-Knowing Prophet reveals His plans to those who seeks Him.

Sets God Apart & Above other gods

In Isaiah 41:23 God challenges the false gods to predict the future and bring it to pass.

Isaiah 41:23 Shew the things that are to come hereafter, that we may know that ye are gods: yea, do good, or do evil, that we may be dismayed, and behold it together.

Isaiah 41:26 Who hath declared from the beginning, that we may know? and beforetime, that we may say, He is righteous? yea, there is none that sheweth, yea, there is none that declareth, yea, there is none that heareth your words.

Confirms Christ's Deity

John 13:19 Now I tell you before it come, that, when it is come to pass, ye may believe that I am he.

God Reveals the Unknown to Seekers

Jeremiah 33:3 Call unto me, and I will answer thee, and shew thee great and mighty things, which thou knowest not.

Pioneer Prophets

These are unique prophets of the Old Testament because they were unlike any of the other prophets of that time. God commissioned them for an exceptional purpose, or they were the first of their kind. For instance, Enoch seems to have been a prophet (Jude 1:14-15). Jude wrote that he prophesied of judgment to come. Enoch is one of only two characters in the

Bible, the other being Elijah, to have been raptured up by God and so avoiding death.

The great-grandson of Enoch, Noah, was also a pioneer prophet. Noah is the only man recorded in the Bible to prophesy of worldwide judgment and see its fulfillment during his lifetime. God told Noah of the global flood and the need to build an ark, which he prophesied of to the people of his time (Genesis 6:8, 13).

Moses was unique both for his calling, and that unlike other prophets of the Old Testament, God spoke to him face to face. Moses was a prophet sent by God to lead the children of Israel out of Egypt. God also gave the people of Israel laws and ordinances through Moses and used him to establish the first covenant with Israel. Unlike other prophets, God spoke to Moses directly, "mouth to mouth."

> *Numbers 12:6-8 And he said, Hear now my words: If there be a prophet among you, I the LORD will make myself known unto him in a vision, and will speak unto him in a dream. My servant Moses is not so, who is faithful in all mine house. With him will I speak mouth to mouth, even apparently, and not in dark speeches; and the similitude of the LORD shall he behold: wherefore then were ye not afraid to speak against my servant Moses?*

Elijah is a pioneer prophet (2 Kings 2:1). He is the only other prophet who escaped death because God supernaturally took him from the earth. During his time, he seems to have stood as the only vocal prophet to the sins of the nation. He confronted the sins of the land from the king's house to the people in a time when Israel had abandoned God, and Baal-worship was common.

Patriarchs

The patriarchs Abraham, Isaac, Jacob, and Joseph all received prophetic revelations and prophesied of things to come. God showed Abraham Israel's future in a vision (Genesis 15:12-16). He told Abraham of the coming fiery judgment on Sodom and Gomorrah by which Abraham interceded and saved Lot and his family (Genesis 18:16-21). Isaac and Jacob both prophesied over their children, and all their prophecies came to pass (Genesis 49). Joseph received a prophetic revelation of his father Jacob and his brothers and prophesied to Pharaoh of Egypt's future. Jacob also prophesied that the people of Israel would leave Egypt.

*Genesis 20:7 Now therefore restore the man his wife; for **he is a prophet**, and he shall pray for thee, and thou shalt live: and if thou restore her not, know thou that thou shalt surely die, thou, and all that are thine.*

Speaking Prophets

As time progresses, God began to call other prophets outside of the pioneers and patriarchs. There were prophets God used in different capacities for certain localities or situations. Aaron, Miriam, Deborah, Nathan, Gad, Micaiah, Samuel, Elisha, Huldah, and many others. These prophets were sent by God through various means to prophesy to the people of the time primarily. The Bible speaks of a "company of prophets" who were speaking prophets. The Bible also speaks of a school of prophets.

Writing Prophets

The writing prophets were contemporary with the speaking prophets. Moses, the model prophet of Israel, wrote the first five books of the Old Testament. Jeremiah, Isaiah, Ezekiel, Daniel are some other examples of the writing prophets. Prophets, who were inspired by God, wrote all the major and minor prophetic books of the Bible. Their prophecies are a part of the canon of Scripture, and are therefore infallible. Not all the prophets of the Old Testament contributed to the Bible. God, in His Sovereign act, used certain prophets to contribute to the Bible, His sacred record.

Lay Prophets

God used men that were not primarily "prophets" in a conventional vocational sense but were used by God prophetically for specific situations. They were not in the office of a prophet, but they prophesied. These were regular men and women that prophesied when the Spirit of God came upon them. They can be called lay prophets. The Spirit of God came upon them:

As Needed

The Spirit of God would come upon some at a moment of need to give a prophetic word. In the following Scripture passage, 2

Chronicles 20, the nation of Israel was facing a threat of war, and God moved Jahaziel to give a word of exhortation and instruction.

2 Chronicles 20:14-15 Then upon Jahaziel the son of Zechariah, the son of Benaiah, the son of Jeiel, the son of Mattaniah, a Levite of the sons of Asaph, **came the Spirit of the LORD** *in the midst of the congregation; And he said, Hearken ye, all Judah, and ye inhabitants of Jerusalem, and thou king Jehoshaphat,* **Thus saith the LORD** *unto you,*

2 Chronicles 15:1-2 And the Spirit of God came upon Azariah the son of Oded: And he went out to meet Asa, and said unto him, Hear ye me, Asa, and all Judah and Benjamin; The LORD is with you, while ye be with him.

By Impartation

God gave to seventy elders of Israel an impartation of the anointing that was upon Moses, and they began to prophesy. Elisha began to function in the prophetic after he received the mantle of Elijah. Later, we will see that through the laying on of hands, believers can receive an impartation of the gift of prophecy.

Numbers 11:25 And the LORD came down in a cloud, and spake unto him, and took of the spirit that was upon him, and gave it unto the seventy elders: and it came to pass, that, when the spirit rested upon them, they prophesied, and did not cease.

By A Company of Prophets

The Spirit of God would come upon others who joined a company or a group of prophets (also called sons of the prophets). This company of prophets initially seemed to have been a school of prophets started by Samuel. The Spirit of God moved upon them to give prophetic utterance.

1 Samuel 10:10-11 And when they came thither to the hill, behold, a company of prophets met him; and the Spirit of God came upon him, and he prophesied among them. And it came to pass, when all that knew him before time saw that, behold, he prophesied among the prophets, then the people said one to another, What is this that is come unto the son of Kish? Is Saul also among the prophets?

1 Samuel 19:20 And Saul sent messengers to take David; and when they saw the company of the prophets prophesying, and Samuel standing as appointed over them, the Spirit of God was upon the messengers of Saul, and they also prophesied.

An Explosion of Lay Prophets

The prophetic revolution taking place today is an explosion of lay prophets. God is still setting up men and women to the ministry office of prophet, but he is also using many lay prophets. These are regular men and women from all walks of life, ages, and culture who the Spirit of God is moving upon to prophesy. They are receiving prophetic revelations and seeing the things to come.

By the Spirit's Outpouring

Continuing into the New Testament when the Spirit of God came upon Elisabeth and Zechariah, they prophesied.

Luke 1:41-42 Elisabeth was filled with the Holy Ghost: And she spake out with a loud voice

Luke 1:67 And his father Zacharias was filled with the Holy Ghost, and prophesied

In the New Testament, the fulfillment of Joel 2:28 begins, which the apostle Peter quoted in Acts 2. The New Testament brings a new utterance – speaking in tongues. At Pentecost when the Holy Spirit came upon the apostles and the 120, they were given utterance in languages unknown to them but known to the hearers. By the same outpouring of the Holy Spirit utterance is given not only in unknown languages (tongues), but in known language (prophecy).

Through the Laying on of Hands

In the scripture below, we see that when Paul laid hands, the believers he was praying for received the Spirit and then spoke in tongues and prophesied.

Acts 19:6 And when Paul had laid his hands upon them, the Holy Ghost came on them; and they spoke with tongues, and prophesied..

By the Spirit's Manifestation

The gift of prophecy is a manifestation of the Holy Spirit. At any time as the need arises, the Holy Spirit can move upon any believer to give prophetic utterance for the benefit of the hearers (1 Corinthians 12:7, 10).

This prophetic revolution is already on the rise. Young, old, male, and female believers around the world are walking in the prophetic in different dimensions. They are proclaiming the soon return of Jesus Christ, giving prophetic utterances as moved by the Spirit, and receiving prophetic dreams and visions.

3

CLARIFYING PROPHETIC TERMS

FOR CLARITY, I will give a short explanation of the prophetic terminology in the book. These are not rigid explanations as the Bible uses prophecy, revelation, the gift of prophecy, prophet, and related terms similarly; they are understood in its context.

Prophecy

Both refer to forth-telling – speaking the mind of God and foretelling – revealing the future. Prophecy can also include revelation of things in the past that was previously unknown for correction, admonition, or warning. Prophecy is the general term used for various forms of revelations and supernaturally given utterance.

Spirit of Prophecy

The Spirit of Prophecy is the Holy Spirit in His operation in all realms of the prophetic that points to the person, work, and glory of Jesus Christ. Also in His function of moving upon men to proclaim and prophesy of Christ, His work, and His coming. This includes the prophecies of Scripture, the anointing to boldly preach the gospel and proclaim the second coming of Christ. In short, the Spirit of Prophecy speaks of Jesus.

Testifies of Jesus

Revelation 19:10 And I fell at his feet to worship him. And he said unto me, See thou do it not: I am thy fellowservant, and of thy brethren that have the testimony of Jesus: worship God: for the testimony of Jesus is the spirit of prophecy.

Moved on the Prophets of Old

2 Peter 1:21 For the prophecy came not in old time by the will of man: but holy men of God spake as they were moved by the Holy Ghost.

Testified Beforehand of Christ

1 Peter 1:10-11 Of which salvation the prophets have inquired and searched diligently, who prophesied of the grace that should come unto you: Searching what, or what manner of time the Spirit of Christ which was in them did signify, when it **testified beforehand** *the sufferings of Christ, and the glory that should follow.*

The Spirit of Prophecy moved the Old Testament prophets to speak in advance of the coming Christ.

Working in the Preaching of the Gospel

1 Peter 1:12 Unto whom it was revealed, that not unto themselves, but unto us they did minister the things, which are now reported unto you by them that have preached the gospel unto you with the Holy Ghost sent down from heaven; which things the angels desire to look into.

The same Spirit who moved the Old Testament prophets to declare the coming Christ anoints believers to preach the gospel today.

The Gift of Prophecy

In its basic form, the gift of prophecy is the manifestation of the Spirit, giving the believer the utterance to speak words of exhortation, admonition, and comfort, in the known language of the hearers. It is the higher form of utterance than the gift of tongues. Speaking in tongues is Spirit-given utterance in an unknown language – unknown by the speaker, and possibly also the hearers. The gift of prophecy is Spirit-given utterance in a known language that is understood by the hearers. It is not merely preaching a sermon, but a supernaturally given utterance. The gift of prophecy can operate with prophetic revelation.

1 Corinthians 12:7, 10 But the manifestation of the Spirit is given to every man to profit withal…to another prophecy

1 Corinthians 14:3-5 But he that prophesieth speaketh unto men to edification, and exhortation, and comfort. He that speaketh in an unknown tongue edifieth himself; but he that prophesieth edifieth the church. I would that ye all spake with tongues, but rather that ye prophesied: for greater is he that prophesieth than he that speaketh with tongues, except he interpret, that the church may receive edifying.

Prophetic Utterance

Prophetic utterance occurs when the gift of prophecy manifests through a person. An utterance is a spoken word. The person speaks in known language as the Spirit supernaturally gives the utterance. Therefore, a prophetic utterance occurs when a person prophesies as the Spirit gives the unction. In the New Testament, the transliteration of the Greek word for "prophesy" is prophéteuó[vi]. It occurs 28 times in the New Testament and usually refers to forth-telling, but can also be about predicting the future.

Acts 19:6 And when Paul had laid his hands upon them, the Holy Ghost came on them; and they spake with tongues, and prophesied.

Prophetic Revelation

A revelation of the past, present, or future that may come through a dream, vision, word of knowledge, word of wisdom, similitude, and other similar revelations. Prophetic revelation is not necessarily spoken at the time it is given, such as in a dream or vision. However, one operating in the gift of prophecy may, at the same time, receive a revelation and utter what they are seeing or hearing from the Spirit of God.

Ministry Office of Prophet

The ministry office of the prophet is the vocational call to be a prophetic speaker for God. It is a ministry gift given to the body of Jesus Christ to equip the saints in the prophetic. The prophet is first a minister of the Word of God in its full counsel, both Old and New Testament, rightly dividing the word (Acts 15:32). Prophets use the Scriptures to reveal the plan of God for the church and address the injustices in society. The uniqueness of the office among the ministry gifts is that the prophet not only expounds on the Bible but also regularly operates in the gift of prophecy and receives multiple prophetic revelations. Some are abusing this ministry gift and proclaiming themselves to be prophets without any accountability. However, not all who prophesy are in the ministry office of the prophet.

Seer

In the Old Testament, the term seer was used in the earlier days of Israel to refer to prophets (1 Samuel 9:9, 2 Chronicles 33:18, Amos 7:12, Micah 3:7). It means one who receives visions. A seer receives from God supernatural revelations of the unknown.

Lay Prophets

The term lay prophets, as used in this book, speaks of regular believers who God uses to prophesy. Lay prophets are not in the ministry office of a prophet. Only some believers are called to the ministry office of the prophet. However, the Holy Spirit can manifest the gift of prophecy through any believer (1 Corinthians 12; 14:24; 14:31). Lay prophets will primarily give prophetic utterances as moved by the Spirit. The person in the ministry office of the prophet is a ministry leader who receives multiple revelations, and gives prophetic utterances more frequently.

Identifying Biblical Prophecies

Prophecy is the most prevalent spiritual gift of the Bible. Prophets wrote more than half of the books in the Old Testament. Moses wrote the first five biblical books. Samuel the prophet likely wrote most of the books named after him. Then you have the seventeen prophetic books from Isaiah to Malachi. Furthermore, Old Testament books that were not written by a prophet also contain prophecies. Altogether, the terms prophet, prophecy, prophesy, and seer occur over five hundred times in the Bible. The prophetic phrase "thus saith the Lord" from the King James Version occurs over three hundred times. At least seventeen of the twenty-seven New Testament books, more than half, contain explicit prophecies. The Bible is prophetic.

In the Bible, a prophecy can be recognized by phrases such as "the word of the Lord came" or "thus saith the Lord," and "prophesied," and other similar expressions. However, prophecy often takes place in the Bible without any of these specific clues. For example, the book of Psalms is filled with prophecies, though often lacking these terms. We recognize the prophecies in Psalms because evidently, the Psalmist speaks about something beyond himself and his time; for example, David prophesied of the Messiah in Psalm 110 calling him Lord. Jesus knowing it was a prophecy questioned the Pharisees saying, *What think ye of Christ? whose son is he? They say unto him, The Son of David. He saith unto them, How then doth David in spirit call him Lord, saying, The LORD said unto my Lord, Sit thou on my right hand* (Matthew 22:43-45). Jesus shows that David was speaking beyond his human understanding; instead, the Holy Spirit was moving David to speak the prophetic words.

Throughout the Bible, as the Spirit of God moved upon people, often they would prophesy. The evidence that an utterance was prophetic is usually due to it revealing something unknown. Furthermore, a prophetic utterance is often spontaneous without the speaker preconceiving the message. Elisabeth spontaneously spoke of Christ the Lord while He was yet in Mary's womb (Luke 1:42-45).

Similarly, as believers stand for God, prophetic utterance will spontaneously flow from their lips. Some will recognize it and say "thus saith Lord" or related phrases, while others will manifest the Spirit of prophecy without realizing it. Growing persecution will take place, and Christians will even be arrested and killed, but those who stand will utter with unconceived words flowing from their lips. Believers will continue to arise with prophetic power, and it will be revolutionary.

4

PROPHETIC COMMODITY

PROPHECY HAS BECOME a commodity in the earth. It's a valuable commodity that cannot be exchanged for money. In its original and simplified sense, commodities are products of value that are widely produced. An example of a commodity is corn. Once the corn is properly grown, its value is the same no matter where it is produced. Corn is grown on every populated continent on earth, so it is widely available. Corn is of immense value since it is used not only for food, but also to produce ethanol, plastic, and hygienic products.

The mass outpouring of the Spirit of Prophecy is having a commodity effect on prophetic utterances and revelations. Prophetic utterances and revelations are becoming widely available, and they are of great value. Like how corn is produced worldwide, God is positioning prophetic voices in every populated continent on the earth.

Corn is a trusted staple even in the worst of times; similarly, the value of prophecy will increasingly become apparent in these times. In a time of the so-called "fake news", misinformation on social media, biased news reporting, propaganda, contradicting statistics and research results, mass accusations, and false conspiracy theories a word from the Lord is needed to have true guidance in society. In this informational overload, prophecy provides a light in the darkness. Believers who walk in this prophetic revolution will have unparalleled clarity and speak with conviction in a dark world.

First, just as corn is widely produced, in this prophetic revolution, prophecy is also being widely produced. Prophetic utterances and revelations are no longer only for the seemingly qualified, such as the clergy or the theological scholar. Instead, prophetic utterances and revelations are given to all who have the testimony of Jesus Christ.

All with the Testimony of Jesus Christ

The testimony of Jesus Christ is the Spirit of Prophecy. Christ holds the key to all prophetic revelation. He unveils the mystery of all prophecies. Surely, He is the first and the last, the Alpha and Omega, the beginning and the end. Therefore, all revelations and knowledge, past, present, and future is in Him. He is the Lamb of God that was found worthy to open the books and the loose the seals (Revelation 5:5); these books unveiled prophetic revelations of the last days.

Therefore, those who have the testimony of Christ have access to hear and see prophetic revelation. Those who have the testimony of Christ can speak a word of prophecy as the Spirit gives them the utterance. Those with the testimony of Jesus Christ can walk in the victory of prophetic fulfillment. Therefore, believers in Christ with the testimony of Jesus Christ, hear what the Spirit is saying, see what the Spirit is showing, and speak as the Spirit gives the utterance.

For the Unexpected

Matthew 13:17 For verily I say unto you, That many prophets and righteous men have desired to see those things which ye see, and have not seen them; and to hear those things which ye hear, and have not heard them

Once you have the testimony of Jesus Christ, the Spirit of Prophecy lives within you. With the coming of Christ, God began to unveil mysteries which were hidden before. However, He did not reveal it to a company of known prophets, or the king's house. God did not seek out the priests. Instead, Christ called common men and women to whom he revealed hidden mysteries. He called those that would not be expected.

When the outpouring of the Spirit came on the day of Pentecost, both men and women were speaking in languages unknown to them as the Spirit gave them utterance. Later, many Gentiles were receiving the same gift of the Spirit. Initially, the apostles did not expect that the Gentiles would receive the Spirit and prophesy. However, the Spirit came upon the Gentiles, and they prophesied.

Surely, among the believers of the first church, there were male and female prophets, and many of the believers of both gender and different backgrounds prophesied. All four daughters of the evangelist Philip prophesied based on *Acts 21:9 And the same man had four daughters, virgins, which did prophesy.*

The mysteries of Christ, His work, and His Second Coming were being received and preached by numerous men and women of different backgrounds. As Jesus stated, even prophets and righteous men wanted to see this and have not been able to. For the church age, the Spirit of Prophecy who spoke through the Old Testament prophets of the coming Christ is now moving upon many believers to proclaim the gospel of Jesus Christ.

1Peter 1:10-12 Of which salvation the prophets have inquired and searched diligently, who prophesied of the grace that should come unto you: Searching what, or what manner of time the Spirit of Christ which was in them did signify, when it testified beforehand the sufferings of Christ, and the glory that should follow. Unto whom it was revealed, that not unto themselves, but unto us they did minister the things, which are now reported unto you by them that have preached the gospel unto you with the Holy Ghost sent down from heaven; which things the angels desire to look into.

For the Unlearned

Luke 10:21 In that hour Jesus rejoiced in spirit, and said, I thank thee, O Father, Lord of heaven and earth, that thou hast hid these things from the wise and prudent, and hast revealed them unto babes: even so, Father; for so it seemed good in thy sight.

The revelation of Christ was not limited to the religiously educated of the time. The revelation of Christ is not limited to the theological scholars, or the experienced clergy but also the babes - the inexperienced, the new believers, the new disciples of Christ. God is now revealing his mysteries to anyone that will hear. All believers in Christ, young and old in the faith, have access to hearing from God. Jesus said, *"my sheep hear my voice"*

(John 10:27). The sheep of Christ are all the real followers of Jesus

All Members of the Body of Christ

1 Corinthians 14:31 For ye may all prophesy one by one, that all may learn, and all may be comforted.

1 Corinthians 14:24-25 But if all prophesy, and there come in one that believeth not, or one unlearned, he is convinced of all, he is judged of all: And thus are the secrets of his heart made manifest; and so falling down on his face he will worship God, and report that God is in you of a truth.

The apostle Paul repeatedly pointed out the importance of the gift of prophecy in the church and emphasized that all believers should desire to manifest the gift of prophecy.

- Desire to Prophesy. *1 Corinthians 14:1 Follow after charity and desire spiritual gifts, but rather that ye may prophesy.*

- All should prophesy because prophecy is greater than speaking in tongues. *1 Corinthians 14:5 I would that ye all spake with tongues, but rather that ye prophesied: for greater is he that prophesieth than he that speaketh with tongues, except he interpret, that the church may receive edifying.*

- All should prophesy because it will convince the unbeliever. *1 Corinthians 14:24 But if all prophesy, and there come in one that believeth not, or one unlearned, he is convinced of all, he is judged of all:*

Unlike the past, the prophetic is no longer for a select few, but God is releasing many to prophesy under the Holy Spirit's power. God's plan is for prophetic voices to be on every continent on earth. All cultures and ethnic groups will have a prophetic witness of Christ and His soon return. While there may be a shortage of hearing the truth, those who walk in prophetic conviction will be a valuable voice in the land. Just as corn has tremendous value and is available worldwide, God has orchestrated that His word can be heard through a worldwide army of prophets.

Why is there then a famine for hearing the Word of God? Because the greats, the well-known, that most people listen to often fail to speak with conviction and prophetic power. Some are just trying to appease to the culture, and retreat from confronting the evils of our time. The prophetic corn is available, but God is raising up the unknown, the pew, to speak the pure gospel with prophetic power.

Amos 8:11 Behold, the days come, saith the Lord GOD, that I will send a famine in the land *of hearing the words of the LORD*:

Jeremiah 5:5 I will get me unto the great men, and will speak unto them; for they have known the way of the LORD, and the judgment of their God: but these have altogether broken the yoke, and burst the bonds.

Compromising with the evils of society causes a famine of hearing God's word. But God is moving upon an unknown remnant of committed believers around the world, who have the prophetic corn. This remnant is on every populated continent on the earth. Through them, abundant corn is being given on the earth.

Psalm 72:16 There shall be an handful of corn in the earth upon the top of the mountains; the fruit thereof shall shake like Lebanon: and they of the city shall flourish like grass of the earth.

5

THE GREAT VALUE OF PROPHECY

MOST PEOPLE KNOW that corn is a staple food, but do not realize that the value of corn goes beyond that. You have likely used a non-food product that was made from corn. Most of the corn produced today are not used for food. Corn is used for ethanol. Furthermore, corn starch and corn syrup are other products of corn. But there is a list of products that are made from corn including breakfast cereals, candies, chewing gum, carbonated beverages, disposable diapers, and more. Corn is a valuable commodity. It is produced on every populated continent on the earth and has multiple uses.

Like corn, prophecy has a wide range of benefits to the church and society. Why did the Apostle Paul emphasize the gift of prophecy? Paul knew that prophecy had great value. It is greater than the gift of tongues. Today, Pentecostal and Charismatic believers usually speak in tongues, just as it seems to have been in the Corinthian church. Among many believers, giving a prophetic utterance is not as common a practice as speaking in tongues. Yet, prophecy has a greater value. Prophesying and prophetic revelation must become the norm among believers as with speaking in tongues. Speaking in tongues has value only for the person speaking it except it is interpreted. But prophesying, and prophetic revelation edify other believers and provide convincing evidence to the world of God's presence. Below, you will find the great value of prophecy.

It Proves the Deity of Christ

John 13:19 Now I tell you before it come, that, when it is come to pass, ye may believe that I am he.

Jesus declared to his disciples that he was telling them revelation of the future so that when it occurs, they would be convinced that He is the Christ. Prophetic revelation provides evidence of the Deity of Christ since only God can consistently speak the future and it accurately come to pass. Lamentations 3:37 declares, *"Who is he that saith, and it cometh to pass, when the Lord commandeth it not?"* Only if it is from the Lord can a thing be spoken, and it comes to pass. Everything else is just guessing. Psalm 33:9 says, *"For he spake, and it was done; he commanded, and it stood fast."* God performs His word, and He knows all things. When a prophecy comes to pass, it proves that God is at work.

Isaiah 41:23 Shew the things that are to come hereafter, that we may know that ye are gods.

God challenged the false gods to prove their deity by shewing the things to come. Of course, false gods cannot accurately predict the future. The same is true for prognosticators from non-Christian religions; they cannot accurately predict the future so that it comes to pass. It may be possible for someone to make a probable guess of the future that occurs. But prophecy from

God is fulfilled beyond the range of what's possible by chance. Therefore, God declared in *Isaiah 45:21*, *"Tell ye, and bring them near; yea, let them take counsel together: who hath declared this from ancient time? who hath told it from that time? have not I the LORD? and there is no God else beside me; a just God and a Saviour; there is none beside me."* He challenges the idol worshippers to look at the matter and see that, only the God of Israel has accurately declared the things to come. Prophecy is of great value because it provides convincing proof of the Deity of Christ.

Our apologetics, the defense of the faith, is often only centered in what can be studied and reasoned logically. This is good and should continue. However, giving prophetic revelation and utterance by the Spirit can provide a supernatural witness of the faith. Furthermore, even an atheist can more quickly understand a prophecy and a fulfillment before our apologetics. The Babylonian king, Nebuchadnezzar, acknowledged the God of Israel when Daniel the prophet interpreted the king's dream, which all the fortune-tellers of the Babylonian kingdom failed to do (Daniel 2). The supernatural manifestation of the prophetic revelation was enough to convince the idol-worshipping king that the God of Israel was greater than all the other gods (Daniel 2:47). When believers allow the Spirit of God to speak through them in their places of influence, it will provide evidence of Christ's deity.

It Convicts of Sins

1 Corinthians 14:24-25 But if all prophesy, and there come in one that believeth not, or one unlearned, he is convinced of all, he is judged of all:

And thus are the secrets of his heart made manifest; and so falling down on his face he will worship God, and report that God is in you of a truth.

The value of prophecy is that an increase in the number of believers that prophesy will bring more of a convicting witness to the unbeliever. The prophetic word will expose the hidden sins of the sinner's heart, showing that God is speaking through His people.

A church worker from New York shared with me her testimony of witnessing to a Rastafarian[vii] taxi driver. The taxi driver claims that he is afraid of church people. However, she began sharing the gospel with him and through the Spirit exposed issues in his life. He confessed to her that the things she was saying, he was just experiencing the same morning. He began to cry. Although he tries to avoid Christians, he remains open to hearing her share the gospel. The prophetic revelation opened the door for the believer to continue sharing the gospel with the Rastafarian.

Think of how Jesus' revelation to the woman of Samaria, the woman at the well, concerning her adulterous lifestyle led her to believe that Jesus was the Messiah. She acknowledged that Jesus was the Messiah saying, *"that he told me all the things I ever did."* Jesus' revelation revealed the secrets of her life and so convinced her that He was the Messiah. Even so, as all believers of the body of Christ prophesy, unbelievers will be convicted of their sins as they see the glory of Christ in the church.

Saves Lives

Before the terrorist attack on the famous Twin Towers of New York City on September 11, 2001, a group of street preachers and evangelists were preaching in the city and warning it of a coming flood of evil upon the land. They were preaching for the people of New York to repent only days before the attack. God always has a witness of things to come so that a way is provided for life to be saved.

The unwilling prophet Jonah was used by God to save the lives of the people of Nineveh. Jonah prophesied to the Ninevites that God would destroy the city because of their wickedness. The people of Nineveh united in repentance and fasting, and God held back judgment on the city. The prophetic word saves lives. The prophet operates as a watchman. When the prophet warns, and the people take heed to the message, they are saved from the calamity to come (Ezekiel 33). God always has a witness when disaster is coming to an area (Amos 3:7-8). He will reveal the matter, and when spoken, it can save the lives of those who hear.

Noah prophesied of the judgment to come upon the whole earth. He built an ark for the saving of lives but only eight responded. God had Noah build the ark to save as many lives as possible. Abraham had a prophetic revelation of the judgment to come upon Sodom and Gomorrah. Abraham interceded for the righteous of the cities, and so succored the safety of Lot and his family.

Lot was warned of the judgment to come and received instruction on how to escape. He escaped with his wife and children while the cities were being destroyed by fire.

Today, God has witnesses in every region of the world who He speaks to concerning the troubles coming upon the land so that people can be warned, and souls can be saved.

Edifies the Church

1 Corinthians 14:3 But he that prophesieth speaketh unto men to edification, and exhortation, and comfort.

God uses the gift of prophecy in the church to give words of encouragement, comfort, and admonition to the people of God. The prophetic word will stir God's people to stand on the promises of God and continue the work of God.

Ezra 6:14 And the elders of the Jews builded, and they prospered through the prophesying of Haggai the prophet and Zechariah the son of Iddo. And they builded, and finished it

In the work of building the church of God, prophecy provides a stirring in the heart of believers to continue doing the work of the Lord until it is completed.

A Signal of God's Revival

Joel 2:28 that has been quoted several times, already shows that prophetic utterance is a signal of revival. A prophetic utterance can stir the people of God to action or call them to repentance. The unction to prophesy coming upon a believer can give boldness to proclaim the word of the Lord, and thus trigger a revival. Once the people of God from all walks of life around the world begins to prophesy, revival fire comes upon the earth. As seen in Ezekiel 37:10, *"So I prophesied as he commanded me, and the breath came into them, and they lived, and stood up upon their feet, an exceeding great army;* prophecy is a trigger for revival.

A Weapon in Spiritual Warfare

Believers can conduct spiritual warfare using prophecy. Prophecy is the doorway to fulfillment. Prophetic revelation reveals the mind of God concerning a matter or warns of adverse situations. And, a prophetic utterance is a driving force to accomplish divine acts. In Christ, all things are fulfilled.

> *And he said, Hearken ye, all Judah, and ye inhabitants of Jerusalem, and thou king Jehoshaphat, Thus saith the LORD unto you, Be not afraid nor dismayed by reason of this great multitude; for the battle is not yours, but God's. To morrow go ye down against them: behold, they come up by the cliff of Ziz; and ye shall find them at the end of the brook, before the wilderness of Jeruel. Ye shall not need to fight in this battle: set yourselves, stand ye still, and see the salvation of the LORD with you, O Judah and Jerusalem: fear not, nor be dismayed; to morrow go out against them: for the LORD will be with you.*
>
> *Hear me, O Judah, and ye inhabitants of Jerusalem; Believe in the LORD your God, so shall ye be established; believe his prophets, so shall ye prosper. And when he had consulted with the people, he appointed singers unto the LORD, and that should praise the beauty of holiness, as they went out before the army, and to say, Praise the LORD; for his mercy endureth for ever. And when they began to sing and to praise, the LORD set ambushments against the children of Ammon, Moab, and mount Seir, which were come against Judah; and they were smitten (2 Chronicles 20:15-22).*

King Jehoshaphat, King of Judah, was about to face a battle against an enemy he could not naturally defeat. After seeking God in prayer, through a prophetic utterance, God released a revelation of what they should do. Jehoshaphat followed the words of the prophecy which said they should present themselves before the enemy, but that they would not need to fight. In obedience, Jehoshaphat sent singers out before the army praising God. The prophetic utterance and the king's obedience ushered a move of God, as the enemy was obliterated before they got to the battlefield. When God gives His prophetic word of promise through a revelation or a prophetic utterance, we can stand on it with praises to God that the battle is won. As a pastor, I have often reflected on given prophecies to stand against current attacks from the devil or to believe God beyond the present circumstance.

I Timothy 1:18 This charge I commit unto thee, son Timothy, according to the prophecies which went before on thee, that thou by them mightest war a good warfare

The apostle Paul charged Timothy to utilize the prophecies that were spoken concerning him to fight a good warfare. When faced with opposition, the prophecies on a person's ministry and gifting is a launching pad to fight against attacks. It is good practice to write down revelations from God to have in memory the prophecies that have been spoken concerning a ministry, or church. In adverse times, they can be spoken as a weapon against opposition.

Gives Direction from Economic Burden

Preparation for Difficult Economic Times

Acts 11:27-29 And in these days came prophets from Jerusalem unto Antioch. And there stood up one of them named Agabus, and signified by the spirit that there should be great dearth throughout all the world: which came to pass in the days of Claudius Caesar. Then the disciples, every man according to his ability, determined to send relief unto the brethren which dwelt in Judaea.

Agabus, the prophet, warned the early church of a coming worldwide famine. In a culture mostly dependent on farming, famine caused a significant downturn in the economic state of society. Scarcity of produce for food would affect all areas of the economy. Through the prophecy, the church prepared for the coming economic plight.

God gave Joseph revelatory interpretation of Pharaoh's dream that there would be seven years of prosperity in Egypt and seven years of worldwide famine. Since Joseph provided the interpretation of the dream, the Pharaoh of Egypt made him the prime minster over Egypt in charge of preparing for the famine to come. Through this, Joseph not only prepared Egypt to be preserved in famine but also his family, the people of Israel, had a safe place amid a scarcity of food throughout the region.

Readiness for Prosperity

2 Kings 7:1-2 Elisha said, Hear ye the word of the LORD; Thus saith the LORD, To morrow about this time shall a measure of fine flour be sold for a shekel, and two measures of barley for a shekel, in the gate of Samaria.

Then a lord on whose hand the king leaned answered the man of God, and said, Behold, if the LORD would make windows in heaven, might this thing be? And he said, Behold, thou shalt see it with thine eyes, but shalt not eat thereof.

Elisha the prophet gave a prophetic revelation of a boost in the economy in Israel. The faith-driven action of four lepers allowed them to reap the benefits of the prophecy. But the unbelieving officer of the king's court died without experiencing the economic uptick because he rejected the prophecy (2 Kings 7:2). Through a prophetic word, the financial status of a person or nation can change for the better.

Prophetic Insight for the Future Generation

Today my oldest son is a preacher of the gospel, and my daughter regularly ministers in song at my church. However, my wife and I saw this before they were born. In a prophetic revelation, my wife saw our first son being delivered while preaching the gospel. For our daughter, the Holy Spirit spoke to my wife, saying that she will sing like an angel. Both our children are today living out these prophecies. The prophetic revelation gave us insight into their future and prepared us for the ministries they would have. We see examples of this throughout the Bible.

1 Samuel 2:1 And Hannah prayed, and said, My heart rejoiceth in the LORD, mine horn is exalted in the LORD: my mouth is enlarged over mine enemies; because I rejoice in thy salvation.

Hannah's prayer of praise to God for delivering her from barrenness and giving her a son, Samuel, speaks of things to come. Hannah uttered insights into the work of God in the coming generations.

The prayer not only gave thanks to God for giving the child Samuel but also prophesies of the future. In the time of Hannah, there was no king in Israel. Yet, in the song of Hannah, she said, *"the Lord shall judge the ends of the earth; and he shall give strength unto his king, and exalt the horn of his anointed."* She speaks of God's anointed king. Hannah could have been prophesying of the coming kings of Israel, but more likely, the Holy Spirit was speaking through her of Jesus Christ the Anointed One. God was revealing the coming Messiah, who also came into the earth through a miraculous birth. Through this prophetic utterance, we see a glimpse into God 's redemptive work in the coming generations.

Luke 1:41-42 And it came to pass, that, when Elisabeth heard the salutation of Mary, the babe leaped in her womb; and Elisabeth was filled with the Holy Ghost: And she spake out with a loud voice, and said, Blessed art thou among women, and blessed is the fruit of thy womb.

Elisabeth, filled with Holy Spirit prophesied of the destiny of Jesus Christ, while he was still in Mary's womb. Through prophecy, God will give insight into the callings and destiny of the future generation.

There is more that can be said about the great value of prophecy. But this sufficiently demonstrates the benefits of receiving and walking in the prophetic gift that God is releasing upon the church today. Let us see how prophecy can operate in your life for making crucial decisions. `

6

PROPHETIC REVELATION FOR LIFE DECISIONS

THE HOLY SPIRIT lives in every believer and guides them in the truth. For direction in making life decisions, God can and will give prophetic revelations to the believer. For the believer to operate in the prophetic, she must attune to the voice of God. While God may, at times, speak in an incredible, undeniable way, most believers learn to recognize God's voice as they daily follow the leading of the Spirit of God. God speaks to His children. God's children are expected to recognize His voice and follow him. Jesus said, *"my sheep hear my voice… and they follow me"* (John 10:27). Furthermore, the believer must be so sensitive to the voice of God that they can detect a strange voice (John 10:5).

Upon salvation, the Holy Spirit enters a person's life and gives an inner assurance of salvation. Romans 8:16 says that *the Spirit itself beareth witness with our spirit that we are the children of God.* The Spirit then guides us into all truth. The Holy Spirit teaches the believer by illuminating the Word of God and leading into righteous living. If we fellowship with God through His Spirit and obey his voice, then we become sensitive to the voice of God. Therefore, the Psalmist admonishes in Psalm 95:7-8, *"To day if ye will hear his voice. Harden not your heart."*. When the heart is open to the voice of God we will be able to recognize His voice.

Distinguishing the Voices

There are many voices in the world that we may hear, and they should not be confused with the voice of God. 1 Corinthians 14:10-11 says *There are, it may be, so many kinds of voices in the world, and none of them is without signification. Therefore if I know not the meaning of the voice, I shall be unto him that speaketh a barbarian, and he that speaketh shall be a barbarian unto me.* Other voices can influence the decisions we make. We must know how to distinguish the voice of God despite the noise. The prophet Elijah had to discern the voice of God despite the distractions.

> *I Kings 19:11-13 And, behold, the LORD passed by, and a great and strong wind rent the mountains, and brake in pieces the rocks before the LORD; but the LORD was not in the wind: and after the wind an earthquake; but the LORD was not in the earthquake: And after the earthquake a fire; but the LORD was not in the fire: and after the fire a still small voice. And it was so, when Elijah heard it, that he wrapped his face in his mantle, and went out, and stood in the entering in of the cave. And, behold, there came a voice unto him, and said, What doest thou here, Elijah?*

When you need to hear from the Lord, you must know how to recognize His still small voice from the sounds and events around you.

The following are some examples of the many different voices that seek to gain our attention.

Human Voice

God can speak to us through others. He uses the voice of human beings to convey his message. However, Christians must be able to discern when the human voice is speaking a word from God. Furthermore, we must determine when it is in God's will to follow a person's voice.

Family and Relatives

The human voice may be speaking from a human perspective or giving a message from God. We must discern the difference. The human voice may come through a spouse, such as the example of Adam and Abraham obeying the voice of their spouse (Genesis 3:17; Genesis 16:2). This may be the voice of a relative such as Moses listening to the voice of his father in law, Jethro (Exodus 18:24). It could be the voice of a parent (Deuteronomy 21:18). In all examples that involve family and relatives, we cannot assume to follow just because of the relationship. Listening to the human voice should be done through the filtering of the Word of God, and the leading of the Spirit. Children should obey their parents in the Lord. Wives should submit to their husbands in accordance with the Word of God.

Man's voice does not equate to the voice of God. When a man is giving a message from God, then his words should be received as coming from the Lord. The first man Adam listened to the voice of his wife disobeying God by eating the forbidden fruit

(Genesis 3:17). Abraham obeyed the voice of his wife to have sex with their maid instead of believing God for the promised child (Genesis 16:2). Both Adam and Abraham should have rejected the voice of their spouse since they were speaking outside of God's will. Personal opinions and conclusions, even when good, should be evaluated as to whether they align with the Word of God and the Spirit of Christ. Reject or rebuke the voice of men when it violates the voice of God. Jesus rebuked Peter, recognizing that he was speaking according to the desires of Satan in Matthew 16:23 saying *But he turned, and said unto Peter, Get thee behind me, Satan: thou art an offence unto me: for thou savourest not the things that be of God, but those that be of men.*

Government

Follow the voice of governmental leaders only under their God-given roles to punish wickedness and preserve civility, not equating them with the voice of God. God killed Herod when the people regarded his voice as the voice of God; God judged Herod because of it (Acts 12:22). Always obey God above the voice of government. The apostles told the religious leaders of Israel, *"we ought to obey God rather than man" (Acts 5:29)*. When the commandments of government violate the voice of God, then we must obey God.

Voice of God's Servants

Isaiah 50:10 Who is among you that feareth the LORD, that obeyeth the voice of his servant

The believer can follow the voice of a true servant of God once as it aligns with the Scriptures. A servant of God is a ministry leader who is accountable for ministering to others, such as a pastor, or any in the ministry gifts (apostle, prophet, evangelist, pastor, teacher). Faithful servants of God will have a credible reputation for godly living, biblical teaching, and principled leadership. A servant of God may preach, teach, prophesy, or provide biblical counseling. When a servant of God speaks according to God's word, God is using the servant of God to bring direction.

The faithful believer will search the Bible to ensure that what a servant of God is speaking is based on Scripture. When it comes to personal prophecy and biblical counseling, the Spirit of God will convict the believer to move in the direction that's in His will or confirm it with an inner assurance. In my experience as a pastor, frequently, when a believer seeks counseling, they already had a nudging from the Spirit towards the wise direction. The counsel of a godly minister often confirms the Spirit's witness to the believer; or otherwise, warns the believer to avoid a direction that the Spirit was already bringing conviction about.

Admonitions to Discern the Voice of Ministers

- ➢ Don't despise true prophecies (1 Thessalonians 5:20).

- ➢ Don't mistakenly reject the sermon, teaching, or counsel of faithful servants of God because of a flaw in their communication. They may use strong words, or they may be soft-spoken, or, they may use terms that you find offensive. It's the agreement of the message with the Word of God that is crucial, not word usage, or personal styles (Isaiah 29:20-21; 2 Corinthians 10:10-11).

- ➢ God will often use the voice of a real servant of God to train you toward recognizing His voice. When Samuel first heard God's voice, he thought it was the voice of the priest Eli (1 Samuel 3). It's not unusual for you to receive revelations that involve a true servant of God in your life. Following the example and instruction of a faithful servant of God will help you to discern God's voice.

Informational/Instructional/Confirmational

- ➢ Preaching and teaching based on God's word are instructional. These are not optional, so faithfully apply them to your life.

- ➢ Prophetic revelations are sometimes informational (of the past, present, or future); Based on the information that is given in a prophecy, then steps must be made according to God's word. The information is not a direction or instruction; rather, it provides knowledge so that an informed decision can be made in line with God's word. One can always seek God for further wisdom in deciding what to do.

- ➢ Prophecies that include instruction or direction must align with God's word, and confirm the Spirit's convicting leading. In this time of grace, it is not God's plan for believers to be directed from others without any confirmation from the Bible and the Spirit who lives within them. You should be able to confirm a prophetic instruction through the Bible and the conviction of the Spirit in your life.

- ➢ Counsel may be instructional – a direct command from Scripture such as the instruction not to marry an unbeliever. Biblical instructions should be obeyed. Counsel may also be a prophetic instruction bringing conviction of an action that must be taken.

- ➤ Counsel may be optional – weighing the risks and rewards of different options based on the wisdom of God's word, prophetic insight, the grace and knowledge given to the servant of God, known spiritual and practical information about your life. However, this type of counsel should not be taken lightly, as the servant of God is often given wisdom from the Spirit of God to guide toward the right path (1 Corinthians 7:25, 40).

- ➤ Reject the word of prophets and ministers who compromise the exclusivity and deity of Christ, gives a license to sin, are bound in sexual immorality, and speaks against Bible-believing churches and true ministers of the gospel (2 Peter 2). These often bring division, and seldom remain faithful to a local church.

Conditional

- ➤ Some prophecies are conditional. The prophecy's fulfillment depends on the action of the person or people who are the subjects of the prophecy. For example, I have received warnings from God of a negative outcome if I remained at a particular place. What I saw in the revelations did not materialize because I moved from the area.

- ➤ The best known biblical example of a conditional prophecy is in the book of Jonah. Jonah prophesied to the city of Nineveh that, *"Yet forty days, and Nineveh shall be overthrown"* (Jonah 3:4). But after forty days the city was not overthrown because the people repented of their sins in fasting. A predicted temporal judgment can be avoided through sincere repentance.

➢ A promise of blessings was spoken over the people of Israel, but it was based on their obedience. They would be blessed if they obeyed God, but experience a curse if they disobey Him (Deuteronomy 28). Even so, many personal prophecies of the future are conditional upon our obedience to God.

Prophetic Answers

God can speak through a servant of God the solution to a problem that you may be having.

Biblical Promises

➢ A servant of God may be more knowledgeable about Scripture verses and promises. He may be able to direct you toward a promise of Scripture for you to hold to for deliverance from the problem.

Revelatory Wisdom

➢ God can reveal the solution to a problem through a servant of God. This is often the word of wisdom in operation. The servant of God see what needs to be done, and the outcome of the action. Examples:

    o Jesus sends Peter to find money in the fish's mouth to pay taxes (Matthew 17:26-27).

    o After Peter failed to catch fishes through the night, Jesus tells Peter to go out deep into the lake and let down his net for a draught of fishes (Luke 5:4-10).

- Elisha's instruction to the woman to borrow as many containers as possible, fill them with the oil she has and then sell it, to pay off her dead husband's debt (2 Kings 4:1-7).

- Interpretation of a dream or vision like when Joseph interpreted Pharaoh dream of the coming prosperity and famine. Then Joseph gave a solution to survive the years of famine.

Ministry Support

➢ God assigns you to support or donate to the ministry of a servant of God. When you face a personal problem, the solution can often come through the servant of God. Essentially, the servant of God can give a solution that increases your ability to continue supporting his ministry. Because you are assigned to the servant of God, when you follow those instructions, it also releases blessings into your life.

Matthew 10:41-42 He that receiveth a prophet in the name of a prophet shall receive a prophet's reward; and he that receiveth a righteous man in the name of a righteous man shall receive a righteous man's reward. And whosoever shall give to drink unto one of these little ones a cup of cold water only in the name of a disciple, verily I say unto you, he shall in no wise lose his reward.

Angel's Voice

Hebrews 2:2-4 For if the word spoken by angels was stedfast, and every transgression and disobedience received a just recompence of reward; How shall we escape, if we neglect so great salvation; which at the **first began to be spoken by the Lord**, *and was* **confirmed unto us by them that heard him;** *God also bearing them witness, both with signs and wonders, and with divers miracles, and* **gifts of the Holy Ghost**, *according to his own will?*

In the Old Testament times, angels gave messages to men. Although this also occurs in the New Testament, it appears to be much less than the Old Testament. With the coming of Christ, God no longer primarily speak through angels, but instead He speaks to us through His Son Jesus Christ by the Holy Spirit. The Holy Spirit will lead the believer. Angels may be sent by God to assist a believer, but it seems to be very rare for an angel to be used to give a message. Any message from what appears to be an angel that is contradictory to the gospel or the Word of God should be rebuked. Moreover, even in cases where an angel speaks a scripture, it may not be God's will at that moment. For example, satan tempted Jesus to make bread when He was fasting; another time, satan quoted a scripture for Jesus to jump off a cliff (Matthew 4:3-6). Furthermore, any message that leads to the worship or adoration of an angel is demonic and should be rebuked sharply.

Galatians 1:8 But though we, or an angel from heaven, preach any other gospel unto you than that which we have preached unto you, let him be accursed.

Colossians 2:18 Let no man beguile you of your reward in a voluntary humility and worshipping of angels, intruding into those things which he hath not seen, vainly puffed up by his fleshly mind,

Inner Thoughts

Ecclesiastes 10:20 Curse not the king, no not in thy thought…for a bird of the air shall carry the voice…

Many people mistake the voice of their inner thoughts for the voice of God. We have many thoughts throughout the day that may be triggered by multiple things – our feelings, an observation, news reports, television, human opinions, etc. The voice of God amid the many thoughts is what gives us comfort as the Bible states in *Psalm 94:19 In the multitude of my thoughts within me thy comforts delight my soul.* Thoughts can come from our carnal desires, and feelings of the body as the Bible states in *Mark 7:21 For from within, out of the heart of men proceed evil thoughts, adulteries, fornications, murders.* The devil may even give suggestive thoughts to our mind. However, we have been given weapons to come against ungodly thoughts that enter the mind. If we entertain an ungodly thought, then it becomes sin. Therefore, we must not confuse the thoughts of the mind with God's voice. Instead, we must cast down all thoughts that are contrary to the will of God, and bring every thought into obedience to Christ using the weapons of the Word of God, prayer, fasting, rebuking, resisting, declaring, and confessing.

The voice of the Holy Spirit will commune with our spirit, and this illuminates the mind. Romans 8:16 says, *"The Spirit itself beareth witness with our spirit, that we are the children of God."* Proverbs 20:27 says, *"The spirit of man is the candle of the LORD, searching all the inward parts of the belly."* Therefore, we must pay attention to the things of the Spirit, God's Word and Work, and reject things of the flesh. Through prayer, fasting, fellowship with the saints, personal evangelism, Bible study and giving we invest in the work of the Spirit which enables us to distinguish the voice of God from the thoughts of the flesh.

Fleshly thoughts that are inspired by the devil will produce works of the flesh such as adultery, fornication, idolatry, witchcraft, heresies, drunkenness, and such the like (Galatians 5:19-21). These may seem obvious, but other works of the flesh include jealousy, envy, strife, rage, divisions, and such the like. The Corinthian church was filled with divisions, and jealousies and so were unable to receive certain things from God. The apostle Paul stated that he had to feed the Corinthian church with milk, and not meat because being carnal they could not handle strong meat. Thoughts that are competitive in seeking personal glory or gain, thoughts that are envious of others, and attempt to put others down are devilish (James 3:13-17).

God's voice will be pure and peaceful. His voice will lead you to walk in purity. His voice will give an inner assurance of peace that this is the will of God. God's voice will direct you to make decisions that are straight, no duplicity or hypocrisy. The voice of God will produce good fruits in your life, fruits of godliness (James 3:17-18).

Voice of a Sign

Exodus 4:8 And it shall come to pass, if they will not believe thee, neither hearken to the voice of the first sign, that they will believe the voice of the latter sign.

A miraculous sign from God is a message within itself. The ultimate sign was the resurrection of Christ. Christ's resurrection was a clear message from God that Jesus is the Messiah (Acts 17:31).

It Shows God's Approval

Acts 2:22 Ye men of Israel, hear these words; Jesus of Nazareth, a man approved of God among you by miracles and wonders and signs, which God did by him in the midst of you, as ye yourselves also know:

It's a Confirming Witness of the Message

Hebrews 2:4 God also bearing them witness, both with signs and wonders, and with divers miracles, and gifts of the Holy Ghost, according to his own will?

The voice of a sign shows God's approval of his servants. It also confirms the message being spoken. God can use miracles in the life of a believer to prove His will. Moreover, God works wonders through us as a witness of His power to others. However, not every miracle or sign is from God, so we must discern the voice of a sign.

Discerning the Voice of a Sign

2 Thessalonians 2:9 Even him, whose coming is after the working of Satan with all power and signs and lying wonders,

A false miracle or sign leads to other gods, another gospel, another Christ, and deceives into following false doctrines. Reject miracles and signs that contradict the Bible, and comes from a person who denies the truth of the gospel.

False miracles resemble true signs but lack divine power and authority. With further investigation and time, it becomes clear that a fake miracle is not a real sign from God. False miracles go beyond the simplicity and purity of devotion to Christ; if it involves actions, steps, devices, concoctions and remedies outside of the name of Jesus, and commitment to Christ, it stems from falsehood. Authentic miracles from God does not require potions, mixes, penance, or "work," but merely the power of Jesus in obedience to God's word.

False miracles lead to the praise of men instead of exalting Jesus Christ; it places the abilities and charisma of the "miracle-worker" over the power of Jesus Christ, and the simplicity of the gospel. It builds allegiance to the man over devotion to Christ.

However, genuine miracles will bring glory to God, confirm the truth, and propel God's work. Believers should expect to experience miracles in their lives such as healing, special favor, supernatural solutions to problems, confirming the promises of God's word. We must also believe God to work miracles through us as a witness of His glory.

Voice of Nature

Nature provides a general revelation of the existence of God. *Psalm 19:1-4 The heavens* **declare the glory of God**; *and the firmament sheweth his handywork. Day unto day* **uttereth speech**, *and night unto night sheweth knowledge. There is no speech nor language, where their* **voice is not heard**. *Their line is gone out through all the earth, and* **their words to the end of the world**. *In them hath he set a tabernacle for the sun,*

Nature is a time marker for acting on God's will for your life. It is best to recognize and act on nature's revelation of God's glory while young, it becomes more difficult with age. Frustration with the imperfection of nature due to the fall becomes more prominent as humans grow older, and skews humankind's perception of nature's declaration of God's glory. This is the thesis of Ecclesiastes 12 to remember God while young before old age, and eventually, death reduces your ability to respond to nature's message.

Additionally, the earth itself continues to decay in corruption; the increasing earthquakes, natural disasters, and diseases are evidence of earth's decay. Therefore, believers should take heed to make the best of their time in doing God's will. The natural aging process on our bodies and the constant decay of the earth should heighten the urgency of doing God's will.

Ecclesiastes 12:1-2 Remember now thy Creator in the days of thy youth, while the evil days come not, nor the years draw nigh, when thou shalt say, I have no pleasure in them; While the sun, or the light, or the moon, or the stars, be not darkened, nor the clouds return after the rain

Nature can communicate coming weather events and impending calamities.

Luke 12:54-56 And he said also to the people, When ye see a cloud rise out of the west, straightway ye say, There cometh a shower; and so it is. And when ye see the south wind blow, ye say, There will be heat; and it cometh to pass. Ye hypocrites, ye can discern the face of the sky and of the earth; but how is it that ye do not discern this time?

But nature's voice does not communicate God's divine purpose, and judgment. Humankind can discover the designs and patterns

God has enacted in nature that brings the realization of God's existence. But humankind must act on God's revelation in Jesus Christ, and through the Bible.

Nature should not be used as a means of spiritual direction or insight. Idolaters and astrologers make this mistake; they try to use nature for spiritual direction. Nature only communicates the glory of God's existence and His designs on the earth. Spiritual revelation comes from the Bible and knowing Jesus Christ.

Satan's Voice

We know that the devil speaks. He spoke to Jesus during Christ's temptation in the wilderness. The devil spoke Bible verses and made suggestions to Jesus. Jesus vehemently rebuked satan even when the devil quoted Scripture.

Characteristics of Satan's Voice:

Questions the Truth of God's Word

Genesis 3:1 Now the serpent was more subtil than any beast of the field which the LORD God had made. And he said unto the woman, Yea, hath God said, Ye shall not eat of every tree of the garden?

Downplays the Consequences of Sin

Genesis 3:4 And the serpent said unto the woman, Ye shall not surely die:

Highlights the Fleshly Benefits of Sin

Genesis 3:5-6 For God doth know that in the day ye eat thereof, then your eyes shall be opened, and ye shall be as gods, knowing good and evil. And when the woman saw that the tree was good for food, and that it was pleasant to the eyes, and a tree to be desired to make one wise, she took of the fruit thereof, and did eat

Twists a Scripture to Deny a Fundamental Truth of God's Word

Matthew 4:6 And saith unto him, If thou be the Son of God, cast thyself down: for it is written, He shall give his angels charge concerning thee: and in their hands they shall bear thee up, lest at any time thou dash thy foot against a stone.

For example, some preachers teach that we are gods, despite the fundamental teaching of Scripture that there is only one God, and we are all his creation. The twisting of one or two scriptures to deny the whole teaching of the Bible is a work of the devil.

Forbidding Marriage

1 Timothy 4:1-3…some shall depart from the faith, giving heed to seducing spirits, and doctrines of devils…Forbidding to marry…

Pushing the Dietary and Ceremonial Laws of Moses as a Requirement for Believers in Christ

I Timothy 4:1-3 …some shall depart from the faith, giving heed to seducing spirits, and doctrines of devils…Forbidding to marry and commanding to abstain from meats…

Accuses and Slanders Believers

Revelation 12:10 for the accuser of our brethren is cast down, which accused them before our God day and night.

Job 1:9-11 Then Satan answered the LORD, and said, Doth Job fear God for nought? Hast not thou made an hedge about him, and about his house, and about all that he hath on every side? thou hast blessed the work of his hands, and his substance is increased in the land. But put forth thine hand now, and touch all that he hath, and he will curse thee to thy face.

Any voice that seeks to speak evil of the true church of God is from the devil. While God will correct sins in a church, He always provides for repentance. But satan's voice will slander a church to cause you to disconnect from a church where God has sent you. Satan will also accuse you of sins of which you have repented to keep you in a state of condemnation. Believe God's word concerning you over the devil's accusation.

Denies that Jesus Christ is God in the Flesh

1 John 4:3 And every spirit that confesseth not that Jesus Christ is come in the flesh is not of God: and this is that spirit of antichrist

Leads to Worship of Entities other than God

Matthew 4:8-9 Again, the devil taketh him up into an exceeding high mountain, and sheweth him all the kingdoms of the world, and the glory of them; And saith unto him, All these things will I give thee, if thou wilt fall down and worship me.

Denial of Sin

I Timothy 4:1-2 Now the Spirit speaketh expressly, that in the latter times some shall depart from the faith, giving heed to seducing spirits, and doctrines of devils; Speaking lies in hypocrisy; **having their conscience seared with a hot iron**

Voice of Wisdom

Proverbs 1:20 Wisdom crieth without; she uttereth her voice in the streets.

Biblical wisdom is walking in the fear of the Lord. Therefore, it is the wisdom of God. The fear of God is to keep his word (Psalm 111:10). Keeping the Word of God is walking in wisdom. We gain wisdom in all matters of life by calling out to God for his voice. *James 1:5 If any of you lack wisdom, let him ask of God, that giveth to all men liberally, and upbraideth not; and it shall be given him.*

Fool's Voice

Ecclesiastes 5:3 For a dream cometh through the multitude of business; and a fool's voice is known by multitude of words.

Contrary to the voice of wisdom, the fool's voice babbles about multiple ideas. From the internet and media, there are many voices and opinions. The fool listens to all the things around him and repeats them. There is no deciphering of the truth nor discernment of the voice of God. Anything or anyone that speaks double is the voice of a fool. That which contradicts the narrow path of God's word is foolish.

How to Hear the Voice of God

A voice from God will never tell you to turn away from Jesus or to honor Him less than God. Accordingly, a voice from God will never lead you to give worship to another being other than our God and Savior Jesus Christ. Therefore, the voice of God will not lead you to equate instructions or teachings from other religions with God's word.

To recognize and become attuned to the voice of God, it begins by applying God's word, seeking His voice, and expecting to hear from Him.

Apply God's Word

James 1:19 Wherefore my beloved brethren let every man be swift to hear, slow to speak, slow to wrath.

James 1:21 Wherefore lay apart all filthiness and superfluity of naughtiness and receive with meekness the engrafted word, which is able to save your souls.

James 1:22 But be ye doers of the word, and not hearers only deceiving your own selves.

Psalm 119:105 Thy word is a lamp unto my feet and a light unto my path.

When you hear and apply God's word you increasingly become sensitive to his voice. God will illuminate the word in your spirit. The entrance of God's word gives light and understanding (Psalm 119:130) and, *the secret of the Lord is with them that fear him (Psalm 25:14)*. The fear of the Lord is to keep his commandments.

Use the Word of God to determine decisions that must be made in life. The Word of God should be the litmus test for every decision that is made. Obey God's word concerning your daily habits, family life, career, ministry, finances, and you will increasingly become sensitive to the voice of God.

Seek His Voice

Proverbs 2:3, 6 Yea, if thou criest after knowledge, and liftest up thy voice for understanding. For the Lord giveth wisdom: out of his mouth cometh knowledge and understanding

Jeremiah 33:3 Call unto me and I will answer thee and show thee great and mighty things which though knoweth not.

Seek the voice of God before you make any life decision. When I was thinking about getting married, I first committed the matter to prayer. Before the Lord, I placed the choices that I was considering at the time. The Lord answered my prayer and showed me who would be my future wife. Today I have been married to her for over twenty years and cannot imagine how anyone else would have been the right companion for me. However, if I had gotten into marriage without a revelation from God, I possibly would have chosen the wrong person. If you seek the voice of God concerning the decisions that you need to make, He will reveal His plan to you.

Expect to Hear

God is Often Speaking

Genesis 3:8 And they heard the voice of the Lord God walking in the garden in the cool of the day.

With every act, God speaks. Adam and Eve would hear the voice of God walking. God's very steps uttered His voice. This is because before God acts, He speaks. Or rather, He performs His word. Therefore, expect to hear from God as you seek Him; He speaks as He works in your life.

Job 33:14-15 For God speaketh once, yea twice, yet man perceiveth it not. In a dream, in a vision of the night when deep sleep falleth upon men, in the slumberings upon the bed.

God will speak to you in a variety of ways. It may be in a vision or dream. God revealed to my wife that I was her husband through a dream. The Holy Spirit may speak to you. God revealed the woman that I would marry by speaking to me through His Holy Spirit. When the church was praying for my then future wife in a prayer meeting, the Holy Spirit said to me, "that is your wife." He may give you a sense of peace in a particular direction. Or the Lord may give you a prophetic word. Expect to hear from God.

His Sheep Hear His Voice

John 10:27 My sheep hear my voice and I know them, and they follow me.

All born again believers are sheep in God's pasture. He is our shepherd and so we should hear his voice. Expect God our Shepherd to lead you in the path of righteousness.

The Spirit Leads Sons of God

Romans 8:14 For as many as are led by the Spirit of God they are the sons of God.

Here is another confirmation that you should expect to hear from God. The Spirit of God leads all of God's children. If the

Holy Spirit does not lead you, then you are not a child of God. The Lord is leading you; listen for His voice.

The Anointing Abides in You

1 John 2:27 But the anointing which ye have received of him abideth in you, and ye need not that any man teach you; but as the same anointing teacheth you of all things, and is truth, and is no lie, and even as it hath taught you, ye shall abide in him.

Don't wait for someone; expect to hear from God. The anointing in you will teach you and lead you into truth.

God Reveals the Hidden Things to us by His Spirit

1 Corinthians 2:9-11…Eye hath not seen, nor ear heard…But God hath revealed them unto us by his Spirit; …the things of God knoweth no man, but the Spirit of God.

His Spirit reveals to us the blessings that we have in Christ Jesus.

His Spirit Bears Witness with Our Spirit

Romans 8:16 The Spirit itself beareth witness with our spirit, that we are the children of God

The Holy Spirit gives us the inner confidence that we are the children of God. He will witness to our spirit about our identity in Christ. Once you are born again, the Spirit of God lives within you and comforts you. So, expect to hear from God.

God Orders Your Steps

Psalm 37:23 The steps of a good man are ordered by the Lord

Through Christ, we have been made righteous. God orders the footsteps of the righteous. God will set the course of your life. Listen to His voice and follow Him.

All these promises of God tell us that we should expect to hear from God. God speaking to His children is the norm, not the exception. Since you are his sheep, since you have His Spirit, since he orders your steps, then with confidence anticipate that God will speak to you.

Follow the Spirit

As you expect to hear from God, He will speak to you by His Spirit. Follow and obey the leading of the Spirit. Whatever the Spirit leads you to do, do it quickly. 1 Thessalonians 5:19 says, *quench not the Spirit*. Do not water down the prompting of His Spirit. Instead, follow His voice.

John 16:13 Howbeit when he, the Spirit of truth, is come, he will guide you into all truth: for he shall not speak of himself; but whatsoever he shall hear, that shall he speak: and he will shew you things to come.

Receive Prophetic Utterances and Revelations

1 Thessalonians 5:20 Despise not prophesying.

God may use a prophet or just a faithful believer to give you a message that can give you clarity in your situation. When God speaks to you through a proven prophet or a committed believer, do not despise it. Receive it.

2 Chronicles 20:20 …Believe in the LORD your God, so shall ye be established; believe his prophets, so shall ye prosper.

Look for Confirmations

2 Corinthians 13:1...In of the mouth of two or three witnesses every word be established.

God often confirms His word. In whatever form God may speak to you, He will often confirm his message to you. Once as a revelation lines up with God's word, you can ensure that you are hearing from God when He repeats the message by different means. God will speak more than once, perhaps in a dream, vision, or by the Holy Spirit (Job 33:13-15). He may confirm the word through counsel from a faithful servant of God (Proverbs 11:14), or through a sermon or prophecy spoken in a church service.

Test and Act

1 John 4:1 Beloved, believe not every spirit, but try the spirits whether they are of God: because many false prophets are gone out into the world.

Once you believe the Lord has spoken to you, then test the message that you have heard, and act on it.

To test the revelation, answer the following questions:

- Have you discerned the voice you are hearing? (refer to the start of this chapter)
- Does it agree with the Bible?
- Has it been confirmed?
- Does it glorify Jesus for who He is? (1 John 4:2)
- Is the source credible?

THE PROPHETIC REVOLUTION

A dream can occur from images and thoughts on the mind from things such as movies, personal desires, or just general activities throughout the day. These are causative dreams. Any message or dream that seems to come from the dead is not of God. If the source of a message is from someone who is living an ungodly life, then reject it. Test the credibility of the message that you are receiving.

> ➢ Does it give peace? A sense of Assurance?

1 Thessalonians 5:21-22 Prove all things; hold fast that which is good. Abstain from all appearance of evil.

When you obey God's word by testing the revelation, He will be faithful in speaking to you. Test all things. Act on what is good. And avoid what seems evil.

God will speak to you on a personal level with prophetic revelation and insight. By faithfully seeking after God, and becoming familiar with His voice through the Bible, and the leading of His Spirit, you will grow more sensitive to His voice. Begin expecting to hear God's voice as you commit yourself to know and seek after Him.

Expecting to hear from God is your entry into the prophetic. Believers who seek to know the voice of God are making the first step into the prophetic revolution. God wants to speak to every one of His children. But not only that, God wants to speak through every one of His children.

7

THE GIFT OF PROPHECY

PROPHECY HAS BEEN a norm throughout the Bible. Whenever the Spirit of God was poured out on somebody, they would receive supernatural utterance. Since every believer has the Spirit of God, it is not surprising that the New Testament teaches that the gift of prophecy is for all Christians. The apostle Paul discusses the gift of prophecy as a manifestation of the Holy Spirit in 1 Corinthians chapters 12, 13, and 14. The gift of prophecy is also mentioned in Romans, chapter 12. The gift of prophecy as a manifestation of the Holy Spirit is different from the ministry gift of prophet spoken of in Ephesians 4:11. The gift of prophecy is for all believers, while to "some" are given the ministry gift of prophet.

The simple gift of prophecy described by the apostle Paul is primarily an utterance gift – speaking in known language as moved by the Holy Spirit. We know this as Paul speaks of it as a gift that benefits the hearers. The prophecy of Joel in Joel 2:28 is that when the Spirit comes upon anyone that they will "prophesy." Peter describes the outpouring of the Spirit on the day of Pentecost as a fulfillment of Joel 2:28. The believers who received the Spirit spoke in other tongues. In essence, this is similar to prophecy in that they received an utterance or a tongue. However, the New Testament came with tongues unknown to the speaker as a sign to unbelievers. The Jews gathered from different nations were bewildered that they heard the wonderful works of God being spoken in their own languages (Acts 2:11). The phenomenon of a person receiving utterance from the Spirit's outpouring is not new and is in line with prophesying. In the New Testament, the gift of prophecy is in language known to the speaker and hearers, while tongues is unknown to the speaker.

Thus, the simplest manifestation of the gift of prophecy is primarily "forth-telling". *1 Corinthians 14:3 But he that prophesieth speaketh unto men to edification, and exhortation, and comfort. 1 Corinthians 14:4 …but he that prophesieth edifieth the church.* However, this "forth-telling" is spontaneous, Spirit-enabled utterance. Just as speaking in tongues is as the Spirit gives the utterance, the gift of prophecy is as the Spirit gives utterance for edification, comfort, and consolation. It's a supernatural manifestation. It is not a naturally produced utterance as in preparing a sermon or exhortation, but a spontaneous bursting forth of words as the Spirit enables.

Therefore, the most basic operation of the gift of prophecy is to speak under the utterance of the Holy Spirit in known language for edification, comfort, and consolation. The simplest manifestation of the gift of prophecy does not necessarily include a revelation of the future or knowledge of things unknown. It may only be a supernaturally given utterance to strengthen, build up, and comfort believers. Revelation of the future or unknown often occurs in the gift of prophecy also, but we will discuss this in the next chapter. All believers can manifest the gift of prophecy regularly as enabled by the Holy Spirit.

The manifestation of the gift of prophecy in supernatural forth-telling has been in operation throughout the Bible. Throughout Scripture, people would prophesy when the Spirit of God came upon them. When the Spirit of God comes upon the person they utter. The following are some examples throughout Scripture of people speaking as the Spirit enables them.

Numbers 11:25 …when the spirit rested upon them, they prophesied, and did not cease.

1 Samuel 10:10 …the Spirit of God came upon him, and he prophesied among them.

1 Samuel 19:20 and when they saw the company of the prophets prophesying, and Samuel standing as appointed over them, the Spirit of God was upon the messengers of Saul, and they also prophesied.

1 Chronicles 12:18 Then the spirit came upon Amasai, who was chief of the captains, and he said, Thine are we, David, and on thy side, thou son of Jesse: peace, peace be unto thee, and peace be to thine helpers; for thy God helpeth thee.

2 Chronicles 20:14-15 Then upon Jahaziel the son of Zechariah, the son of Benaiah, the son of Jeiel, the son of Mattaniah, a Levite of the sons of Asaph, came the Spirit of the LORD in the midst of the congregation; And he said, Hearken ye, all Judah, and ye inhabitants of Jerusalem, and thou king Jehoshaphat, Thus saith the LORD unto you…

2 Chronicles 24:20 And the Spirit of God came upon Zechariah the son of Jehoiada the priest, which stood above the people, and said unto them, Thus saith God, Why transgress ye the commandments of the LORD, that ye cannot prosper? because ye have forsaken the LORD, he hath also forsaken you.

2 Chronicles 15:1-2 And the Spirit of God came upon Azariah the son of Oded: And he went out to meet Asa, and said unto him, Hear ye me, Asa, and all Judah and Benjamin; The LORD is with you, while ye be with him; and if ye seek him, he will be found of you; but if ye forsake him, he will forsake you.

Luke 1:41-42 … and Elizabeth was filled with the Holy Spirit. And she cried out with a loud voice and said,

Luke 1:67 And his father Zacharias was filled with the Holy Ghost, and prophesied

2 Samuel 23:2 The Spirit of the LORD spake by me, and his word was in my tongue.

Acts 19:6 And when Paul had laid his hands upon them, the Holy Ghost came on them; and they spake with tongues, and prophesied.

Different Administrations of the Gift of Prophecy

1 Corinthians 14:13-17 Wherefore let him that speaketh in an unknown tongue pray that he may interpret. For if I pray in an unknown tongue, my spirit prayeth, but my understanding is unfruitful. What is it then? I will pray with the spirit, and I will pray with the understanding also: I will sing with the spirit, and I will sing with the understanding also. Else when thou shalt bless with the spirit, how

> *shall he that occupieth the room of the unlearned say Amen at thy giving of thanks, seeing he understandeth not what thou sayest? For thou verily givest thanks well, but the other is not edified.*

The gift of prophecy can manifest though various forms of ministering. 1 Corinthians 14 shows that the gift of prophecy can manifest in prayer, singing, thanksgiving, and teaching. Paul instructs the Corinthians to not only speak in tongues when praying, singing, and giving thanks, but to also do them in understanding. One can sing, pray, and praise with understanding by speaking in their ordinary language, or through an interpretation of tongues (making it equal to prophecy). The point of 1 Corinthians 14 is to excel in prophecy over speaking in tongues. Paul continues by saying, *"I had rather speak five words with my understanding, that by my voice I might teach others also, than ten thousand words in an unknown tongue"* (1 Corinthians 14:19). Again, through the gift of prophecy he can speak to others with understanding. The gift of prophecy can manifest in different administrations.

Below, find out more about some of the ways that the gift of prophecy can manifest.

Poetry or Song

Music usually accompanies prophetic ministry. The company of prophets, that were under Samuel's tutelage, prophesied with musical instruments (1 Samuel 10:5). Therefore, a believer can prophesy through a song or hymn. During prayer, worship, or during a church service, the Holy Spirit may give a prophetic song. Prophetic messages can also be repeated in a song.

THE PROPHETIC REVOLUTION

Many of the Psalms of David are prophetic utterances that were given in a song. A psalm is a hymn or a sacred song. 2 Samuel 23:1-7 gives one of the later Psalm of David. 2 Samuel 23:2 says *The Spirit of the LORD spake by me, and his word was in my tongue.* The Psalms of David were often prophetic utterances. David was a prophet according to *Acts 2:29-31,*

> *Men and brethren, let me freely speak unto you of the patriarch David, that he is both dead and buried, and his sepulchre is with us unto this day. Therefore* **being a prophet**, *and knowing that God had sworn with an oath to him, that of the fruit of his loins, according to the flesh, he would raise up Christ to sit on his throne; He seeing this before spake of the resurrection of Christ.*

In the scripture above, the apostle Peter was quoting Psalm 16, which is another song or poem of David, titled "a miktam of David" in many Bible translations. (a miktam is a poetic writing).

King David understood the power of prophetic music and singing. David and his army commanders arranged musicians who would minister prophetically.

1 Chronicles 25:1 Moreover David and the captains of the host separated to the service of the sons of Asaph, and of Heman, and of Jeduthun, who should prophesy with harps, with psalteries, and with cymbals:

The sons of Asaph would prophesy accompanied by musical instruments.

1 Chronicles 25:3 Of Jeduthun: the sons of Jeduthun; Gedaliah, and Zeri, and Jeshaiah, Hashabiah, and Mattithiah, six, under the hands of their father Jeduthun, who prophesied with a harp, to give thanks and to praise the LORD.

These musicians sang prophetic songs to worship God and to exhort the hearers. We are aware of some of the songs they were associated with due to the titles of the Psalms. Psalm 39, 62, and 77 all have the heading to the chief musicians Jeduthun.

In Exodus 15, Moses sang a song of victory after God brought Israel over the Red Sea and overthrew the armies of Egypt. The song was also sung by Miriam the prophetess as she led the women of Israel into praising God. This was a prophetic song of the ultimate victory of the kingdom of God over the power of darkness. A modified version of the song is sung in Revelation 15 showing its prophetic significance. *Revelation 15:3 And they sing the song of Moses the servant of God, and the song of the Lamb, saying, Great and marvellous are thy works, Lord God Almighty; just and true are thy ways, thou King of saints.*

Another song of Moses prophesied of Israel's rebellion and the coming judgment. Deuteronomy 31:30 says, *And Moses spake in the ears of all the congregation of Israel the words of this song, until they were ended.* This song began in Deuteronomy 32; God gave Moses a prophetic song for the nation of Israel (Deuteronomy 31:19-22). It prophesies of Israel's rebellion and God's judgment upon them. The words of the song are prophetic and written as if the events have already happened. God gave Moses the song as a testimony of His faithfulness towards Israel. One of the reasons why God gives prophetic songs is so that it can serve as a memorable witness of the prophecy. *Deuteronomy 31:21 And it shall come to pass, when many evils and troubles are befallen them, that this song shall testify against them as a witness; for it shall not be forgotten out of the mouths of their seed.*

The song of the vineyard is a prophecy spoken by Isaiah (Isaiah 5). Isaiah prophesied that Israel is like a vineyard that should be bringing forth fruits of justice and righteous, but instead brought forth oppression. Isaiah prophesies of God's judgment on Israel due to this.

Today, God is still giving prophetic songs. Jesus Culture Music has done many live performances with prophetic utterances delivered in singing. They believe that God uses their music to ignite revival. The Holy Spirit spontaneously gave some of their songs during their singing and worship[viii]. In December of 2017, the Harvest Army Singers released a song that was given by revelation called "God's Revival is in the Land."[ix]

Through song, God releases prophecies of revival, judgment, victory, and thanksgiving. Believers can prophesy in a song. The gift of prophecy can manifest in a prophetic song during worship, prayer, or in a music ministry in the church. Musicians should allow the Spirit of God to use them to set at atmosphere that is conducive to prophetic utterance.

Prayers

Many prophetic utterances came while a person was praying. Believers can prophesy while praying. Habakkuk's prayer in Habakkuk chapter three is a prophetic prayer. It includes a prophecy of revival and renewal for the people of Israel (Habakkuk 3:2,17-19). Through the prayer, God was releasing prophetic words through the mouth of Habakkuk.

The thanksgiving prayer of Hannah for her son Samuel contains prophetic utterances such as, "*the Lord will judge the ends of the earth,*" and he will "*exalt the horn of his anointed*" (1 Samuel 2:10).

Many of the prayers of the Psalms are prophetic. For example, Psalm 22 seems to be a prayer of David in his ordeal; however, the Psalm is a clear prophecy of the Messiah's suffering on the cross. The following verses show precise fulfillment in Jesus' experience while on the cross: *"they pierced my hands and my feet. I may tell all my bones: they look and stare upon me. They part my garments among them, and cast lots upon my vesture"* (Psalm 22:16-1). On the cross the hands and feet of Christ were pierced, not one of his bones were broken, and they did gamble over his garments. In Matthew 27:45, we can see that Jesus spoke the word that begins Psalm 22, *"My God, My God, why hast thou forsaken me."* We can imagine that during David's time of prayer, God would speak through him prophetically.

While in prayer, God may give prophetic messages and revelations for the individual, the church, or for the world. For example, on April 9th, 2019, while at home in prayer a prophetess from my church received a series of prophetic messages that she wrote; it was then verified and published worldwide. Some of them are below:

> *Have I not given unto you all things pertaineth unto life and godliness; I have given to you all that you need to get the job done, saith the Lord*
>
> *I have relieved you of that burden, I have made provision for all, saith the Lord.*
>
> *I have separated you unto Myself. Live that separated life in the earth", saith the Lord.*

> *I will do a work in your days that will cause your ears to tingle, saith the Lord.*
>
> *The cloud is already bending and I am about to pour out upon you, saith the Lord".*

Believers can expect to hear and utter prophetic words while they are praying. Many Pentecostal and Charismatic believers who pray in tongues can expect the interpretation so that they can pray with prophetic understanding. The Holy Spirit will aid us in prayer by causing us to pray prophetically and speak revelations of the answer.

Praise

Many of the songs and the prayers already mentioned contained prophetic praise. God will give prophetic utterance when his people are praising him.

When the Spirit was poured out on the day of Pentecost as the believers in the upper room spoke in other tongues, the people heard them giving praise to God, speaking of His wonderful works. *Acts 2:11 we do hear them speak in our tongues the wonderful works of God.* They received utterance to speak of God's awesome works in a language unknown to them. Similarly, God gives His people utterance to speak of His wonderful works in a known language.

Preaching and Teaching

The preaching of John the Baptist was without doubt prophetic. When he was preaching and baptizing unto repentance, his message changed as the Pharisees and Sadducees approached him. He said, "*O generation of vipers, who hath warned you to flee from the wrath to come*" (Matthew 3:7). Then he prophesied of the one who would baptize with Holy Ghost and fire (Matthew 3:11).

During a sermon, the gift of prophecy can operate through the preacher, so that he speaks supernaturally concerning a matter or topic with words that he did not preconceive or naturally improvise. Beyond the clergy, believers can expect the gift of prophecy to manifest through them while sharing the gospel through preaching and witnessing.

Many of the Old Testament prophecies were corrections, warnings, and exhortations. The preacher can minister through the manifestation of the gift of prophecy so that his preaching is beyond the norm; instead, his words are Spirit-enabled utterance. To be clear, I am not saying that preaching and teaching is the gift of prophecy; but that, while preaching or teaching, the gift of prophecy can manifest with supernatural utterance. The following scripture in Acts demonstrates this further.

Acts 15:32 And Judas and Silas, being prophets also themselves, exhorted the brethren with many words, and confirmed them

Since the scripture specifically mentions that they were prophets who encouraged the brethren with "many words," without a doubt through the ministry of Judas and Silas their exhortations included prophetic utterances as given by the Spirit. Note also that exhortation is one of the chief outcomes of the gift of prophecy (1 Corinthians 14:3).

Counsel

The Spirit of God is called the Spirit of counsel (Isaiah 11:2). During Old Testament times, people often sought divine counsel. God rebuked the rebellious children of Israel for seeking counsel but not from His Spirit (Isaiah 30:1). In fact, in those times, competent counsel and advice were often considered to be from God. For example, the Scriptures speak of one of David's counselors in this manner: *And the counsel of Ahithophel, which he counselled in those days, was as if a man had inquired at the oracle of God: (2 Samuel 16:23).* We can conclude from this, that it was expected that one could receive counsel from the oracles of God. Oracles are words from God.

God often gave counsel to the kings of Israel through prophetic utterance or prophetic revelation from a prophet. Through a prophetic utterance, King Jehoshaphat of Judah received counsel that he would not need to fight in an upcoming battle (2 Chronicles 20). Through a prophetic revelation, Elisha would warn the king of Israel of the locations where the enemy would attack.

Through a prophecy, Elijah gave counsel to the woman of Zarephath about her last meal saying, "*...thus saith the LORD God of Israel, The barrel of meal shall not waste, neither shall the cruse of oil fail, until the day that the LORD sendeth rain upon the earth" (I Kings 17:14).* Spirit-filled pastors when giving counsel will, at times, speak through the manifestation of the gift of prophecy concerning a matter. Furthermore, the spiritual counselor may receive prophetic revelation. Counselors can minister to others with supernatural utterance and insight from the Spirit of

Prophecy. Believers can give supernatural counsel to others by the gift of prophecy; counsel given through the gift of prophecy can amaze the unbeliever.

The fundamental manifestation of the gift of prophecy is supernatural utterance given to a person to edify, exhort, and comfort. God can use any form of ministering, especially vocal ministry, through which to manifest the gift of prophecy. Poetry, songs, preaching, teaching, counseling, prayer, and praise are all vocal administrations through which the gift of prophecy can flow.

In this prophetic revolution, believers can walk in the enrichment of prophetic understanding in prayer and praise. Flowing in the Spirit, they can preach the gospel of Christ in the public square with prophetic utterances that stings the hearts of men. Even in the marketplaces, neighborhoods, and community centers, God will use believers to give beneficial counsel through the gift of prophecy, giving glory to God. The prophetic Christian consistently spits life-giving fire from their lips through prayer, song, praise, poetry, preaching, and counsel. Expect God to use you through the gift of prophecy in these areas. Next, we will discuss prophetic revelation, and then how to receive the gift of prophecy.

8

PROPHETIC REVELATION

ALTHOUGH MANY BELIEVERS think of prophecy as predicting the future, prophecy includes forth-telling and foretelling. As we have seen, biblical prophecy is not limited to predicting the future, but involves correction, admonition, warning, encouragement, and even revelation of things in the past or present. Forth-telling is proclaiming a message from the Lord. The gift of prophecy, as described in 1 Corinthians 14, is a vocal gift and primarily involves "forth-telling". The apostle Paul described it as a gift in which one speaks to men for *edification, exhortation and comfort* (1 Corinthians 14:3).

However, the gift of prophecy can involve revelations of the past, present, or future. Foretelling is predicting the future. Foretelling is prophetic revelation. Foretelling can occur through the gift of prophecy; this would be a "higher" level of prophecy because revelation is flowing through a prophetic utterance. In other words, prophetic utterance becomes the vehicle by which God delivers the revelation.

Prophetic revelation can be given without the manifestation of a prophetic utterance (1 Corinthians 14:29-32). A person may publicize a revelation that was previously given by a vision, dream, or by the Spirit's voice without the manifestation of prophetic utterance taking place. The revelation can be written or spoken in a normal way. God may cause the speaker to utter the revelation supernaturally; in this case, the revelation is flowing through prophetic utterance.

Often in most Pentecostal or charismatic church services, most people operating in the gift of prophecy are forth-telling under the utterance given by the Holy Spirit. While not exclusively, those in a ministerial office, prominently prophets, often receive prophetic revelation of unknown facts in the past, present or future for the church and society. However, God does give prophetic revelation for the public to lay prophets, regular believers who are committed to hearing from him. Surely, all believers can receive revelation for personal guidance as was discussed in chapter 6. Furthermore, God can manifest revelatory gifts in the life of any believer for the benefit of the church.

Revelation through Dreams and Visions

Joel 2:28 And it shall come to pass afterward, that I will pour out my spirit upon all flesh; and your sons and your daughters shall prophesy, your old men shall dream dreams, your young men shall see visions:

Numbers 12:6 And he said, Hear now my words: If there be a prophet among you, I the LORD will make myself known unto him in a vision, and will speak unto him in a dream.

God often seems to give prophetic revelations through visions and dreams. It is clear from Joel 2:28 that revelations through visions and dreams would be common. We see that this is one of the effects of the pouring out of the Spirit upon all people. God will give prophetic revelations to believers young and old through dreams and visions. Born again believers can expect God to speak to them in visions and dreams.

Revelation through the Voice of God

Numbers 12:7-8 My servant Moses is not so, who is faithful in all mine house. With him will I speak mouth to mouth, even apparently, and not in dark speeches; and the similitude of the LORD shall he behold: wherefore then were ye not afraid to speak against my servant Moses?

However, God can also give revelations through His voice. God spoke to Moses in an audible, external voice. It seems others could even hear God's voice as He spoke to Moses if they were in his presence. This type of audible revelation was limited. In the New Testament, God freely speaks to us by His Spirit and can give revelations by speaking to us through the Holy Spirit. This is not an audible external voice as in the past, but by the inward witness of the Spirit (John 14:17; Romans 8:14, 16; 1 John 2:27). While God can give revelations today through an audible external voice, it is infrequent and less necessary since all believers have the Spirit of God living within them. Born again believers should expect for God to release prophetic revelation by His Spirit into their spirit.

Next, we will look at two biblical examples of prophetic revelation.

Nathan Uttered the Revelation to David

> *2 Samuel 12:7-12 And Nathan said to David, Thou art the man. Thus saith the LORD God of Israel, I anointed thee king over Israel, and I delivered thee out of the hand of Saul; And I gave thee thy master's house, and thy master's wives into thy bosom, and gave thee the house of Israel and of Judah; and if that had been too little, I would moreover have given unto thee such and such things. Wherefore hast thou despised the commandment of the LORD, to do evil in his sight? thou hast killed Uriah the Hittite with the sword, and hast taken his wife to be thy wife, and hast slain him with the sword of the children of Ammon. Now therefore the sword shall never depart from thine house; because thou hast despised me, and hast taken the wife of Uriah the Hittite to be thy wife. Thus saith the LORD, Behold, I will raise up evil against thee out of thine own house, and I will take thy wives before thine eyes, and give them unto thy neighbour, and he shall lie with thy wives in the sight of this sun. For thou didst it secretly: but I will do this thing before all Israel, and before the sun.*

Nathan spoke the revelation of David's sins with all the details and prophesied of what would occur in David's house due to his sin. This was a prophetic revelation of the past sin, present condition, and future consequences. Note that this revelation was given to Nathan for an individual. From the biblical record, the revelation was not announced to the public, only spoken to David.

It seems Nathan's assignment was in the king's household. We have no record of Nathan prophesying to the nation of Israel as a whole. Rather, all the records show that God mainly spoke to him concerning the king's house, and what the king should do.

Agabus prophesied of famine to come

Acts 11:28 And there stood up one of them named Agabus, and signified by the spirit that there should be great dearth throughout all the world: which came to pass in the days of Claudius Caesar.

Agabus gave a prophetic revelation of a famine to come. This revelation was of a global event. It was spoken to the church, and word of it was publicized as much as was possible (Acts 11:27-30). Agabus was recognized as a prophet in the early church. We have references of him giving prophetic revelation to the church, and to ministry leaders.

Lay Prophets and the Scope of Prophetic Revelations

Prophets seem to have different assignments that determine the scope of the prophetic revelations that they most often receive. Remember from chapter two, that lay prophets are regular believers, not appointed to a ministerial office, who God uses prophetically. Every believer can be a lay prophet. The scope of revelations given to lay prophets will often be in the following areas.

Personal (John 10:27; 16:13). This can be for spiritual growth, direction, and guidance in life. This is for every believer.

Family (Matthew 2:13-15; 19-21). For example, God revealed to Joseph how to hide Jesus from the threat of Herod. In His care, God will give prophetic revelations to his people of things happening within the domain of their family.

Local Church (1 Corinthians 14:26-33; 1 Corinthians 11:4-5). It is clear from the early church that there were lay prophets that shared or acted on revelations that God gave to them. God will do this according to the need.

Evangelistic (Revelation 19:10). God will reveal to his people who are faithful in sharing Christ and preaching the gospel, unknown facts in the lives of sinners. God will do this to give convincing evidence to the sinner of the truth of the gospel message, and to give the preacher an open door to reach the sinner's heart and conscience.

These are the primary areas where God will usually give revelation to a lay prophet. However, these are not exclusive. When needed, God can use any committed believer to give prophetic revelations to the body of Christ, nations, political leaders, and the world. Later in chapter ten, we will explore the scope of prophetic revelations given to ministers in the office of a prophet.

Next, we will look at revelatory spiritual gifts found in the Bible that are a form of prophetic revelation. Keep in mind that the revelatory spiritual gifts can operate through any believer as God sees fit. In addition, revelatory spiritual gifts usually manifest in prophecy. The Bible does not distinguish between the gifts stringently because they frequently operate together. As discussed earlier, in its simplest manifestation, the gift of prophecy is Spirit-moved utterance. God can give prophetic revelations through prophetic utterance. Prophetic revelations can also come through visions, dreams, and the Spirit without utterance taking place. We will look at some of the revelatory spiritual gifts and how they operate.

The Gifts of Interpretation

Supernatural interpretation is a form of prophetic revelation

Interpretation of Tongues

1 Corinthians 12:10 ..to another the interpretation of tongues:

1 Corinthians 14:5 I would that ye all spake with tongues, but rather that ye prophesied: for greater is he that prophesieth than he that speaketh with tongues, except he interpret, that the church may receive edifying.

1 Corinthians 14:27 If any man speak in an unknown tongue, let it be by two, or at the most by three, and that by course; and let one interpret.

The interpretation of tongues is an utterance gift given to give the meaning of a vocal message spoken through the gift of tongues. Interpretation is giving the meaning or explanation of something, not a translation. A message given in unknown tongues is of less significance than a prophetic utterance since the public does not understand what is being spoken. However, when the manifestation of the interpretation of tongues takes place, it is equal to a prophetic utterance. Anytime a message is given in tongues, the church should pray for the interpretation. Without the manifestation of the interpretation of tongues, a public message in tongues is of little value to the church.

Interpretation of Dreams

Daniel 5:12 Forasmuch as an excellent spirit, and knowledge, and understanding, interpreting of dreams, and shewing of hard sentences, and dissolving of doubts, were found in the same Daniel, whom the king named Belteshazzar: now let Daniel be called, and he will shew the interpretation.

Daniel 2:28 But there is a God in heaven that revealeth secrets, and maketh known to the king Nebuchadnezzar what shall be in the latter days. Thy dream, and the visions of thy head upon thy bed, are these;

Daniel 2:30 But as for me, this secret is not revealed to me for any wisdom that I have more than any living, but for their sakes that shall make known the interpretation to the king, and that thou mightest know the thoughts of thy heart.

Genesis 40:8 And they said unto him, We have dreamed a dream, and there is no interpreter of it. And Joseph said unto them, Do not interpretations belong to God? tell me them, I pray you.

Genesis 41:15-16 And Pharaoh said unto Joseph, I have dreamed a dream, and there is none that can interpret it: and I have heard say of thee, that thou canst understand a dream to interpret it. And Joseph answered Pharaoh, saying, It is not in me: God shall give Pharaoh an answer of peace.

God often gives revelations through a dream. However, the meaning of a dream is not always clear. A dream has much less value to the dreamer and others if the meaning is unknown. Understanding God's message through a dream cannot be analyzed with human logic and reasoning. It requires supernatural revelation for the meaning of a dream to be understood. Without the Spirit's direction, even the apostle Peter struggled to understand a vision he received from the Lord (Acts 10:9-48).

Therefore, God gives revelation of the meaning of a dream. Through prayer, the dreamer can receive the meaning of a dream from God. However, some believers will manifest the gift to interpret dreams and visions more frequently than others. Daniel seems to have especially been gifted in this area. Believers can seek the Lord in prayer for God to give the meaning of a dream they have received. Since the Holy Spirit lives within every believer, God can give an understanding of the dream's meaning. The goal is not to translate every element in the dream, but to receive revelatory knowledge of the dream's meaning.

Interpretation of Symbols

In Daniel 5, King Belshazzar of Babylon sees a hand writing on the wall (Daniel 5:5-29). He calls the wise men and astrologers of his kingdom, but they could not interpret the writing. Obviously, there was something about the written language that the king, wise men, and astrologers of Babylon could not decipher. There was something revelatory about the written language, and it would take divine revelation to interpret it.

While we rarely, if ever, see symbolic apparitions such as these in our time, symbols will often occur in visions and dreams. The gift upon Daniel to interpret dreams and visions included an understanding of revelatory symbols. It takes supernatural revelation to determine the meaning of symbols in dreams, visions, and other types of revelations.

Interpreting Dreams and Visions

Any believer can receive a dream or a vision from the Lord. At times, the revelation may be clear. Other times, they may include symbols that are difficult to understand. The first thing for believers to do is to ensure that the revelation is from the Lord. Any dream or vision that contradicts the teaching of Scripture is not from God. Additionally, you can dream a dream from your own heart or mind. Something that is heavily upon your heart or a recent event on your mind can be seen in a dream. Many people dream of things that are like a movie that they recently watched. If a dream is filled with recent events and desires of the heart, then most likely the dream is a production of your thoughts, not a revelation from the Lord.

Often the Spirit of God will impress a burden or assurance upon your heart that the dream or vision is from the Lord. Once you know the dream is from the Lord, pray and seek for God's understanding. God may reveal the meaning by speaking to you clearly by his Spirit. He may lead you to a scripture that opens your understanding of the dream's meaning. Through the leading of the Spirit, the symbols of the dream can be understood. God will often use symbols that you are familiar with in your daily knowledge – things we know that would convey the meaning to us. You can increase your symbolic dictionary by studying the ways God usually speak to you, common symbols of Scripture, and improving your knowledge of places and things. For example, learning the map and geographical makeup of different nations may allow God to use geographic features to reveal happenings in a country.

God may also use biblical symbols. Many of the biblical meanings of symbols should be applied in the same manner today. Biblical symbolism is beyond the subject of this book[xi], but as you seek the Lord, His Spirit will use the Scriptures and your common knowledge for you to understand dreams and visions.

Furthermore, remember that some ministers and believers are gifted in this area. If you are still unsure of the meaning of a dream or vision, then share the revelation with a minister of the gospel. If you know someone who frequently operates in prophetic revelations, then share the dream or vision with them. God may give them a revelation of the meaning to share with you. If all else fails, remember that you are a child of God, and God intends to speak to you. If you do not understand his revelation through a dream or vision, God will bring you clarity of the matter through other means.

Other Revelatory Gifts of 1 Corinthian 12

The gifts of the Spirit listed in 1 Corinthians 12 can manifest through any believer as the Spirit of God seems fit. Though they will occur more often through certain ministry offices, God can manifest through anyone with these gifts as needed.

Beyond the gift of prophecy and interpretation of tongues, among the manifestations of the Spirit listed in 1 Corinthians 12, three gifts seem to be revelatory.

Word of Knowledge

1 Corinthians 12:8 For to one is given by the Spirit the word of wisdom; to another the word of knowledge by the same Spirit;

First, let us look at the word of knowledge. Note that this gift is the manifestation of a "word" of knowledge as translated in the King James Version. Other translations such as New International Version use the term "message" of knowledge, and the English Standard Version translates it "utterance" of knowledge. Word, message, utterance all shows that this gift is the manifestation of a revelation given by the Lord. It is a word from the Lord. This word contains knowledge that is known to God. The text in 1 Corinthians 12 does not describe the gift in detail, but we can carefully look throughout Scripture to understand how this gift operates. From a brief survey of Scripture, we can conclude that the word of knowledge is (1) revelation of God's working and plans among His people (Isaiah 11:2-3; Ephesians 1:17; Colossians 1:9; Romans 11:32-34); and, (2) knowledge of the actions and intentions of people (or things connected to people) in relation to God's work.

Knowledge of God's Work Among His People

Numbers 24:16-17 He hath said, which heard the words of God, and knew the knowledge of the most High, which saw the vision of the Almighty, falling into a trance, but having his eyes open, I shall see him, but not now: I shall behold him, but not nigh: there shall come a Star out of Jacob, and a Sceptre shall rise out of Israel, and shall smite the corners of Moab, and destroy all the children of Sheth.

Ultimately, Balaam did not walk in the will of God, but we know this is a true prophecy, and we can gain some general insight from it. The scripture states that he heard the words of God, and knew the knowledge of the most high. Balaam received a word of knowledge. He got a Word of God's working among his people. Specifically, Balaam saw that through Israel, the Messiah would come. Through the word of knowledge, one can receive a word of what God's call and purpose is in the life of a person or group of people. In the body of Christ, many testify of receiving assurance of their ministry calling through a revelation from a prophet or other ministerial leaders. Here Balaam received the revelation in an open vision. A word of knowledge can come through an open vision or dream, as God reveals his working in the lives of His people.

God's wondrous works are perfect in His knowledge. We cannot naturally fathom it. Through the Spirit's manifestation, God gives a glimpse of His workings among his people; this is a word of knowledge. For example, God often reveals His plan for a person's life. In the church at Antioch, the prophets and teachers in the church learned through the Spirit that it was time to send off Paul and Barnabas in the ministry to which they were called (Acts 13:1-3). Without revelation, they would not have had knowledge of this need. I have had the experience of God revealing His plan to use a young child in the ministry. Other times, God has even revealed His plan to use a person who is about to receive Christ. This is God giving knowledge of His plan in the life of a person.

Knowledge of God's Plans in Adverse Circumstances

Job and his friends did not know what was taking place in the spiritual realm as Job endured his trials. Job's friends spoke wrongly of Job. Job spoke beyond his level of understanding. God addressed their ignorance, and said, *Who is this that darkeneth counsel by words without knowledge* (Job 38:2). Job realized that the workings of God's purpose and counsel in the earth, and among His people are too wonderful for the natural mind to grasp (Job 42:3). Understanding of the wonderful workings of God can only come through revelation. Therefore, one aspect of the word of knowledge is when God gives the revelatory understanding of His work among the saints during adverse circumstances..

Knowledge of Actions Related to God's Work

Jeremiah 11:18-19 And the LORD hath **given me knowledge of it***, and I know it: then thou shewedst me their doings. But I was like a lamb or an ox that is brought to the slaughter; and I knew not that they had devised devices against me, saying, Let us destroy the tree with the fruit thereof, and let us cut him off from the land of the living, that his name may be no more remembered.*

Jeremiah knew nothing of a plot to take his life (Jeremiah 11:19). However, God revealed the plot of his enemies to him (Jeremiah 11:18). The word of knowledge is God giving knowledge of the actions of people toward His work. This can be knowledge of good and evil actions. God knows everything about every person. According to Psalm 139, God knows our movements, motives, meditations, imaginations, and every moment of our lives. This depth and abundance of knowledge is far beyond the capacity and understanding of the human mind (Psalm 139:6). For the furtherance of His work, God will give a word of knowledge concerning the movements, motives, or moments in a person's actions. God had more work for the prophet Jeremiah to do, so He revealed the plot to kill Jeremiah. To preserve the sanctity of the newly started church in Jerusalem, the Holy Spirit gave knowledge of the lie of Ananias and Sapphira about the money they were giving (Acts 5). A pastor may receive a revelation of the intentions of members in the congregation so that he may make wise decisions in working with them.

Through the works of Christ, we have an example of the word of knowledge as Jesus revealed information of the Samaritan woman's many husbands (John 4:17-18). Another example is knowing that Nathaniel was a Jew without guile (John 1:47).

Through revelation from the Lord, the blind prophet Ahijah knew that the wife of King Jeroboam came to visit him even though she was disguised (I Kings 14:4-6). Guiding Saul to become the first king of Israel, the prophet Samuel through revelation told Saul where to find his lost donkey.

The word of knowledge goes beyond intellectual knowledge. Furthermore, it is not just salvation knowledge. Rather, it is a supernatural manifestation of the Spirit in the body of Christ. The manifestation of the word of knowledge is for the furtherance of God's work, to the benefit of God's people. This is not just God giving information to people. It will always be revelation to advance God's work and benefit His people.

Word of Wisdom

Wisdom is related to knowledge. Knowledge is needed to act in wisdom. Wisdom is the proper application of knowledge. Through a brief biblical survey, we can conclude that the word of wisdom is revelation (1) to accomplish a task for the advancement of God's kingdom; and (2) to understand what to do at a particular time.

Wisdom to Accomplish a Task

God, in His unparalleled wisdom, made the heavens and established the earth (Psalm 136:5; Jeremiah 10:12). The variety of creatures and their interconnection in nature are all a showcase of God's wisdom (Psalm 104:24). God supernaturally imparts a glimpse of His wisdom so that we may do his work well.

Exodus 28:3 And thou shalt speak unto all that are wise hearted, whom I have filled with the spirit of wisdom, that they may make Aaron's garments to consecrate him, that he may minister unto me in the priest's office.

Exodus 31:3-5 And I have filled him with the spirit of God, in wisdom, and in understanding, and in knowledge, and in all manner of workmanship, To devise cunning works, to work in gold, and in silver, and in brass, And in cutting of stones, to set them, and in carving of timber, to work in all manner of workmanship.

The Spirit of God endowed these men with wisdom to design the priestly garments, and to make the items of the tabernacle. Although they may have had the natural knowledge to design and craft items, only with divine wisdom could they work according to the instruction God had given to Moses. It takes spiritual insight to act effectively on a spiritual revelation. They could only design the materials to Moses's specification through revelation, since the specifications came from the mind of God. As needed, God will impart supernatural wisdom to the saints to accomplish the work of God according to His divine will.

Deuteronomy 34:9 And Joshua the son of Nun was full of the spirit of wisdom; for Moses had laid his hands upon him: and the children of Israel hearkened unto him, and did as the LORD commanded Moses.

Joshua led Israel into the promise land only through divinely given wisdom. The word of wisdom can manifest to give insight into accomplishing a role or an office for the furtherance of God's kingdom. The role may be to serve in a local church or to go on a mission trip overseas; a regular believer will do things beyond their understanding through the manifestation of the word of wisdom.

Wisdom to Understand the Times

Daniel 2:20-23 Daniel answered and said, Blessed be the name of God for ever and ever: for wisdom and might are his: And he changeth the times and the seasons: he removeth kings, and setteth up kings: he giveth wisdom unto the wise, and knowledge to them that know understanding: He revealeth the deep and secret things: he knoweth what is in the darkness, and the light dwelleth with him. I thank thee, and praise thee, O thou God of my fathers, who hast given me wisdom and might, and hast made known unto me now what we desired of thee for thou hast now made known unto us the kings matter.

God's revelation to Daniel was filled with knowledge and wisdom. Knowledge of the contents of the king's dream, and wisdom to know its meaning and application to the king, letting the king know that God was showing him things to come. This wisdom from the Lord was manifested again in Daniel 4, as Daniel interpreted another dream from Nebuchadnezzar and gave him counsel on what to do (Daniel 4:27). The manifestation of the word of wisdom will often include revelation of the future to give clarity on what to do now.

Like Daniel, we see the work of wisdom operated in the life of Joseph, a patriarch of Israel. Pharaoh, king of Egypt, had a dream of events that would happen in Egypt. Joseph was called to interpret the dream. Through revelation from the Lord, Joseph interpreted the dream, and gave counsel to Pharaoh on what to do. The interpretation of the dream was that Egypt would have seven agriculturally prosperous years, and then seven years of famine. Joseph counseled Pharaoh to place a wise man over the affairs of Egypt to save food in the time of prosperity in preparation for the time of famine. Pharaoh acknowledged the wisdom which God had given Joseph, and so made Joseph ruler in Egypt to manage the storage of the food in the plenty years in preparation for the famine (Genesis 41:25-44). This word of wisdom to Joseph was the vehicle by which God brought Joseph into fulfilling his destiny as one of the patriarchs of Israel.

The word of wisdom is two-fold. It is the manifestation of the Spirit, when the Lord gives the knowledge and ability to accomplish a God-given task or assignment. Also, it is the manifestation of the Spirit, giving a glimpse of the future or the unknown, so that we may know what we should do at a given time or situation.

Discerning of Spirits

1 Corinthians 12:10 To another the working of miracles; to another prophecy; **to another discerning of spirits***; to another divers kinds of tongues; to another the interpretation of tongues:*

The discerning of spirits is another revelatory gift. The name of this gift is self-explanatory. Basically, it is the manifestation of the Spirit to distinguish whether a work or message is from the Spirit of God or another spirit. 1 John 4:1 states *Beloved, believe not every spirit, but try the spirits whether they are of God: because many false prophets are gone out into the world.* Since there are false prophets and deceiving wonders, the discerning of spirits benefits the body of Christ because it distinguishes between different types of spirits that are at work.

Micaiah the prophet recognized through revelation that a lying spirit was operating through the prophets who falsely gave Ahab hope of victory in an upcoming war (2 Chronicles 18:17-22).

Elisha was clearly able to recognize supernaturally the presence of angelic spirits surrounding him (2 Kings 6:16-17). Paul recognized the spirit that was operating through Elymas the sorcerer who was seeking to pervert the Word of God (Acts 13:4-12). Paul also recognized the spirit of divination that was operating through the damsel that followed them in Macedonia, declaring that they are servants of God (Acts 16:16-18).

Through the discerning of spirits, God reveals the spirit that is at work in a message or a work. It may be the revelation of unclean spirits at work. It may also be a revelation of the work of angels. When the gift of discerning of spirits is in operation, one can recognize the Holy Spirit's manifestation in different ministries and gifts.

The revelatory gifts of the Spirit often work together. We speak of them separately only to increase our understanding of them, but in operation, many of these gifts operate together. God is giving his prophetic revelation as He pours his Spirit upon all. In a world that is increasingly hostile to Christianity, believers on the frontline of preaching the gospel will receive prophetic revelation to finish the task of reaching the world for Christ.

9

HOW TO RECEIVE THE GIFT OF PROPHECY

THE GIFT OF PROPHECY flows from the outpouring of the Holy Spirit (Joel 2:28). Prophesying is a natural manifestation of the Holy Spirit coming upon the life of the believer. Throughout the Old and New Testament, it is evident that when the Holy Spirit comes upon a person, utterance takes place. In the Old Testament, when the Holy Spirit came upon someone, they would speak out aloud. In the New Testament, utterance occurs in unknown tongues along with prophecy. This is a sure thing in the Word of God. The power of the Holy Spirit coming upon a person brings utterance. Coming up, you will see scriptures that confirm that prophesying is a natural manifestation of the outpouring of the Spirit.

> THE POWER OF THE HOLY SPIRIT COMING UPON A PERSON BRINGS UTTERANCE.

Scriptural Proofs: The Spirit's Outpouring Manifests Prophetic Utterance

Numbers 11:25 ...took of the spirit that was upon him, and gave it unto the seventy elders: and it came to pass, that, when the spirit rested upon them, they prophesied, and did not cease.

Numbers 11:26 ... and the spirit rested upon them; and they were of them that were written, but went not out unto the tabernacle: and they prophesied in the camp.

1 Samuel 10:6 And the Spirit of the LORD will come upon thee, and thou shalt prophesy with them,

1 Samuel 10:10 And when they came thither to the hill, behold, a company of prophets met him; and the Spirit of God came upon him, and he prophesied among them.

1 Samuel 19:20 And Saul sent messengers to take David: and when they saw the company of the prophets prophesying, and Samuel standing as appointed over them, the Spirit of God was upon the messengers of Saul, and they also prophesied.

1 Samuel 19:23 and the Spirit of God was upon him also, and he went on, and prophesied, until he came to Naioth in Ramah.

2 Samuel 23:2 The Spirit of the LORD spake by me, and his word was in my tongue.

1 Chronicles 12:18 Then the spirit came upon Amasai, who was chief of the captains, and he said, Thine are we, David, and on thy side, thou son of Jesse: peace, peace be unto thee, and peace be to thine helpers; for thy God helpeth thee. Then David received them, and made them captains of the band.

2 Chronicles 24:20 And the Spirit of God came upon Zechariah the son of Jehoiada the priest, which stood above the people, and said unto them, Thus saith God, Why transgress ye the commandments of the LORD, that ye cannot prosper? because ye have forsaken the LORD, he hath also forsaken you. 2 Chronicles 15:1-2 And the Spirit of God came upon Azariah the son of Oded: And he went out to meet Asa, and said unto him, Hear ye me, Asa, and all Judah and Benjamin; The LORD is with you, while ye be with him; and if ye seek him, he will be found of you; but if ye forsake him, he will forsake you.

Ezekiel 11:5 And the Spirit of the Lord fell upon me and said unto me, Speak.

Joel 2:28 And it shall come to pass afterward, that I will pour out my spirit upon all flesh; and your sons and your daughters shall prophesy,

Micah 3:8 But truly I am full of power by the spirit of the LORD, and of judgment, and of might, to declare unto Jacob his transgression, and to Israel his sin.

Luke 1:41-42 And it came to pass, that, when Elisabeth heard the salutation of Mary, the babe leaped in her womb; and Elisabeth was filled with the Holy Ghost: And she spake out with a loud voice, and said

Luke 1:67 And his father Zacharias was filled with the Holy Ghost, and prophesied,

Acts 19:6 And when Paul had laid his hands upon them, the Holy Ghost came on them; and they spake with tongues, and prophesied.

The above scriptures clearly demonstrate that the Spirit's outpouring naturally brings prophetic utterance. If the Holy Spirit coming upon a person causes prophetic utterance, then why do we not see this regularly today? First, in the New

Testament God gave the gift of tongues. The gift of tongues is utterance but in an unknown language. This was meant to be a sign of the Holy Spirit's power in the New Testament (1 Corinthians 14:21-22). While the gift of tongues is a vital part of the life of the Spirit-filled believer, prophecy is of greater benefit to each believer, and for the body of Christ. Many believers speak in other tongues by the power of the Holy Spirit.

However, the gift of tongues is not the only or final form of utterance that God wants the believer to operate in regularly. Thinking of it as a film, the gift of tongues is like an opening act; prophecy is the ongoing live-action production. As was the norm from the Old Testament, it is God's plan for the believer to commonly prophesy. Prophesying is the natural outbreak of the Holy Spirit coming upon the believer. Have you already experienced the baptism of the Holy Spirit with the evidence of speaking in other tongues and possibly other spiritual gifts? If yes, then prophetic utterance can naturally flow through your lips as enabled by the Spirit.

> THE GIFT OF TONGUES IS LIKE AN OPENING ACT; PROPHECY IS THE ONGOING LIVE-ACTION PRODUCTION.

It is simple to receive the gift of prophecy to speak in a known language if you have already received the gift of tongues to speak in unknown languages. In the same way that you received the Spirit and spoke in tongues, if you reach out to God by faith He will empower you to prophesy. If you have never experienced the baptism of the Holy Spirit, you can also receive by faith and speak in unknown languages and prophesy (Acts 19:6). Below, there is a layout of how to get in the right disposition to receive the gift of prophecy.

How to Receive

Exalt Christ

1 Corinthians 12:3 Wherefore I give you to understand, that no man speaking by the Spirit of God calleth Jesus accursed: and that no man can say that Jesus is the Lord, but by the Holy Ghost.

The testimony of Jesus is the Spirit of Prophecy. As such, the gift of prophecy will exalt the Lord Jesus Christ. To receive the gift of prophecy, we must exalt Jesus Christ as who He is – God in the flesh.

Having a compromised position on the Personhood of Christ will obstruct the gift of prophecy; in fact, seeking for the gift without exalting Christ as fully God will bring about a counterfeit spirit.

Exalt Jesus Christ as Lord and God; this will set the atmosphere for the Spirit of Prophecy to flow through you. Take the time to reflect on Christ's personhood and work of redemption and give him thanks, praise and worship for who He is. The Spirit of God will testify of Christ, and glorify Him through you.

Desire it

1 Corinthians 14:1 …desire spiritual gifts, but rather that ye may prophesy

1 Corinthians 14:39 …Covet to prophesy…

God commands the church to desire spiritual gifts, but especially prophesying because of its great benefit to the church. Again, the apostle Paul says to covet to prophesy. Covet here means to be zealous over it, and earnestly desire it. God commands us to desire the gift of prophecy zealously. God promises us that when we hunger and thirst after righteousness, we will be filled (Matthew 5:6). When we desire a message from God to pour from our lips, God will fill our mouths with His words.

Through **earnest prayer and fasting**, express to God your desire for the gift of prophecy. When we earnestly seek after the gift in fasting and prayer, God will grant us the gift (Luke 11:11-13).

Psalm 81:10 …Open thy mouth wide and I will fill it.

We ought not to be shy about receiving the gift of prophecy. It is not a matter to wait and see. Now, we must enthusiastically and earnestly seek after God to fill our mouth with His word. If we strongly desire it, God will fill our mouths with His prophetic word.

Sanctify yourselves for it

Jeremiah 15:19 Therefore thus saith the LORD, If thou return, then will I bring thee again, and thou shalt stand before me: and if thou take forth the precious from the vile, thou shalt be as my mouth: let them return unto thee; but return not thou unto them.

God called upon Jeremiah to return to him, to repent, and separate from vile things. God was calling upon Jeremiah to put him first before others and to separate from evil works. If Jeremiah would do this, God said that Jeremiah would be as His mouth; in other words, Jeremiah would be God's spokesman, a prophet.

If we desire to speak God's message, then we must let him sanctify us.

- ➤ Repent of any sin.
- ➤ Commit to being separated from worldliness.
- ➤ Be ready to speak boldly.

Gather in a Prophetic Company

1 Samuel 10:5 …and it shall come to pass, when thou art come thither to the city, that thou shalt meet a company of prophets coming down from the high place with a psaltery, and a tabret, and a pipe, and a harp, before them; and they shall prophesy:

1 Samuel 10:10 And when they came thither to the hill, behold, a company of prophets met him; and the Spirit of God came upon him, and he prophesied among them.

Connect with a prophetic church or ministry that demonstrates the fruits of righteousness and truth. Among a prophetic group of people, the manifestation of the gift of prophecy flows freely. A company of prophets embraces biblical prophecy, watches for the signs of the times, consistently prophesy with accurate fulfillments; and overall, a group of people who encourages the prophetic unction. As seen in 1 Samuel 10:5, music is often a large part of prophetic manifestation. So even during a worship service among a prophetic group of people the power of God can come upon you to prophesy.

Receive it Through the Laying on of Hands

Acts 19:6 And when Paul had laid his hands upon them, the Holy Ghost came on them; and they spake with tongues, and prophesied.

When the apostle laid his hands upon the believers, they received the Holy Spirit and began to prophesy. You can receive the gift of prophecy when a servant of God who is filled with the power of the Holy Spirit and embraces the gift of prophecy lays hand upon you. Allow a godly living servant of God to lay hands on you, and release your faith to prophesy!

Build Faith with Biblically-Based Prophecies

Jeremiah 23:28-29 The prophet that hath a dream, let him tell a dream; and he that hath my word, let him speak my word faithfully. What is the chaff to the wheat? saith the LORD. Is not my word like as a fire? saith the LORD; and like a hammer that breaketh the rock in pieces?

Develop your Prophetic Literacy by learning about the prophecies of the Old Testament that have been fulfilled, especially the prophecies concerning Jesus Christ. Learn them and be ready to speak them. Then study the prophecies of the New Testament concerning the last days, and the signs of Christ's second return. (Study Chapter 14 on Prophetic Literacy). Doing this will build your faith for prophesying.

Furthermore, follow the prophecies of proven prophetic ministries. A prophetic ministry is proven if the ministry is Bible-based, holds to the foundational doctrines of the Christian faith, demonstrates fruits of godly living, and consistently prophesies accurately with observable fulfillments. Witnessing prophetic ministry in action will move your faith to prophesy.

Prophesy

As you seek for the gift of prophecy, believe the Lord, open your mouth wide, and allow God to fill your mouth with his message. As the message bubble within you from the Spirit of God, and the power of God comes upon you, speak boldly without fear. Acknowledge that you are receiving a message from the Lord with *thus saith Lord*, or *the Lord says*, or *the Holy Spirit says*, or *I am receiving a word from the Lord*, etc. Without adding anything, only speak what the Spirit is moving you to say; as the Spirit gives the utterance speak by faith. Go ahead and prophesy, the Lord is bringing a message through you.

How to Stir the Gift of Prophecy

Most believers who speak in tongues, do not prophesy. However, the gift of prophecy is more profitable to the body of Christ than the gift of tongues. Therefore, we need to build our faith to prophesy. As you seek to prophesy, take the following steps to build your confidence and stir the gift in your life.

1. **Memorize the "Scriptural Proofs: The Spirit's Outpouring Manifests Prophetic Utterance"**. Go back to the start of this chapter and memorize at least three of those scriptural proofs that demonstrate that the outpouring of the Spirit brings prophetic utterance.

2. **Privately Pray in Tongues with Interpretation of Tongues**. Practice to speak in tongues in your personal prayer life and expect God to give you the interpretation

3. of the tongues. You can ask the Lord to grant you the interpretation so that you can pray with understanding (1 Corinthians 14:13-15). The interpretation of tongues is equal to a prophetic utterance. The Holy Spirit will give the understanding of the tongues if you desire it.

4. **Repeat Proven Prophecies**. Declare the prophecies of proven prophetic ministries. Find a proven prophetic ministry, and when they publicize a prophecy, declare it to others.

5. **Become Prophetically Literate** (check Chapter 14).

6. **Prophesy to Close Associates**. Pray for close relatives and friends, believing that God will speak prophetically through you into their lives. You may begin by praying for them in tongues, but ask God for the interpretation and prophesy as the Spirit moves you.

10

THE MINISTRY OFFICE OF PROPHET

THE FOCUS OF this book is the manifestation of the Spirit of prophecy through every believer. The prophetic revolution is the mighty rise of lay prophets, the everyday born-again believer, to prophesy under the unction of the Spirit. Albeit, the prophetic revolution will necessarily include men and women being called into the ministry office of prophet.

Four Dimensions of Prophetic Ministry

Prophetic Preaching

Every believer should operate in this dimension. The Spirit of Prophecy will operate in the life of Christ-loving saints to preach the gospel and proclaim Christ's soon return. The gospel of Jesus Christ is prophetic. The Word of God is prophetic. Therefore, the proclamation of the gospel and the preaching of the Word of God is prophetic.

Prophetic Utterance

The gift of prophecy in its most basic manifestation is the unction to utter a message by the Spirit in a language known to hearers. Beyond mere preaching, the believer receives supernatural utterance. All believers who receive the gift of the Holy Spirit can operate in the gift of prophecy. The manifestation of prophetic utterance is available to all believers.

Prophetic Revelation

This is revelation of unknown facts in the future, past, or present. It is the manifestation of revelatory gifts to make known the unknown through visions, dreams, or by prophetic utterance. Based on Joel 2:28, we can see that in this time of prophetic revolution, revelations will take place on a larger scale among believers than in the past.

Prophetic Ministry Office

While in some capacity all believers can operate in the Spirit of Prophecy, not all believers are called to the ministry office of prophet. The person in the prophet's office will operate in the dimensions of prophetic preaching, prophetic utterance, and prophetic revelation frequently and in a greater capacity. Furthermore, these dimensions of prophecy operate through the prophet as a leader who has the responsibility of equipping the body of Christ to do the work of the ministry (Ephesians 4:11-12).

The Prophet

The prophet is a ministry gift written of in *Ephesians 4:11 And he gave some, apostles; and some, prophets; and some, evangelists; and some, pastors and teachers;* Not everyone that has the gift of prophecy is a prophet. All can prophesy, but we are not all prophets. *1 Corinthians 12:27-29 Now you are the body of Christ, and members in particular. And God hath set some in the church, first apostles, secondarily prophets, thirdly teachers, after that miracles, then gifts of healing, helps, governments, diversities of tongues. Are all apostles? Are all prophets? Are all teachers? are all workers of miracles?*

The ministry office of prophet is given only to some to equip the saints and edify the body of Christ. Consequently, the prophet has a crucial role in this prophetic revolution in imparting and equipping the saints to operate in the prophetic dimension. We will look through the Scriptures to understand the office of the prophet, and his role in the prophetic revolution.

Old Testament Prophets

Spokesmen for God

The Old Testament prophets were Spirit-filled spokesmen for God. Micah 3:8 says, *But truly I am full of power by the spirit of the LORD, and of judgment, and of might, to declare unto Jacob his transgression, and to Israel his sin.* Describing the nature of his ministry, Micah the prophet states that he was full of power by the Spirit to declare unto the children of Israel their sin. He was Spirit-empowered to correct God's people. The prophet was compelled to speak God's message as described in Amos 3:8,

The lion hath roared, who will not fear? the Lord GOD hath spoken, who can but prophesy?

Correcting sin, warning the people, and declaring the things to come, the Old Testament prophets spoke as oracles of God, and their messages aligned with God's laws (2 Kings 17:13). They were giving prophetic utterances and revelations by the inspiration of the Holy Spirit. Amos, among the first Old Testament prophets with a book, has the term "saith the Lord" forty-three (43) times with only eight chapters. His declarations included correction of sin, calls for repentance, and prophecy of impending judgment.

Seers

The Old Testament prophets often had supernatural sight through visions (Isaiah 30:10). The term 'seer' was synonymous with prophet (2 Kings 17:13). The message of the prophets was often based on what they saw. For example, Amos 1:1 says, *"the words of Amos,...which he saw concerning Israel...;"* and Obadiah 1:1, *"the vision of Obadiah. Thus saith Lord God,"* and Micah 1:1, *"The word of the Lord that came to Micah...which he saw concerning..."* The seers received multiple visions, and similitudes. Similitudes are similes that God gave to the prophets to convey a message. At times similar to parables, God would show the prophet an image or likeness of something.

Hosea 12:10 I have also spoken by the prophets, and I have multiplied visions, and used similitudes, by the ministry of the prophets.

In the Old Testament, it can be surmised that being seers distinguished the office of the prophet from those who only gave prophetic utterances. The seer would see supernaturally.

Saul, the first king of Israel, was not a seer, but twice prophesied when the Spirit of God came upon him (1 Samuel 10:10; 19:24). David prophesied, and gave revelations of the future in his prophecies, therefore David is called a prophet. *Acts 2:29-31 Men and brethren, let me freely speak unto you of the patriarch David, that he is both dead and buried, and his sepulchre is with us unto this day. Therefore being a prophet, and knowing that God had sworn with an oath to him, that of the fruit of his loins, according to the flesh, he would raise up Christ to sit on his throne; He* **seeing this before** *spake of the resurrection of Christ.* Therefore, it seems that one of the differences between a prophet, and the one who only gives prophetic utterances, is that the prophet tends to have more supernatural revelations such as visions.

The New Testament Prophet

Like the Old Testament prophets, New Testament prophets are also spokesmen for God, and seers. The prophet not only operates in the gift of prophecy to utter, but also in the revelation gifts, such as word of wisdom, word of knowledge, and discerning of spirits.

From what is recorded in the New Testament we can glean some further insights into the office of the prophet in the New Testament.

Preachers of the Word

Acts 15:32 And Judas and Silas, being prophets also themselves, **exhorted the brethren with many words,** *and confirmed them.*

Acts 15:25-27 It seemed good unto us, being assembled with one accord, to send chosen men unto you with our beloved Barnabas and Paul, Men that have hazarded their lives for the name of our Lord Jesus Christ. We have sent therefore Judas and Silas, **who shall also tell you the same things by mouth.** -

The New Testament prophet is a preacher of the word. He preaches to exhort the people of God to walk in the truth of God's revealed word. They confirm through proclamation the truth of the gospel. Acts 15:27 shows us that Judas and Silas, who were prophets, were sent to be a voice of truth to the Gentile believers. They were to preach the same things that the council in Jerusalem had already decided by the Spirit. The true New Testament prophet will not speak contrary to the gospel message but will confirm and establish it. The prophet speaks God's truth with clarity.

The words of Judas and Silas also encouraged and strengthened the brethren (Acts 15:32). New Testament prophets will build up the church through their preaching and utterance. Aligning with Paul's description, the gift of prophecy is utterance for *"edification, exhortation, and comfort"*.

. Operates in Prophetic Revelation

Acts 11:27-28 And in these days came prophets from Jerusalem unto Antioch. And there stood up one of them named Agabus, and signified by the spirit that there should be great dearth throughout all the world: which came to pass in the days of Claudius Caesar.

Acts 21:9-11 And the same man had four daughters, virgins, which did prophesy. And as we tarried there many days, there came down from Judaea a certain prophet, named Agabus. And when he was come unto us, he took Paul's girdle, and bound his own hands and feet, and said, Thus saith the

Holy Ghost, So shall the Jews at Jerusalem bind the man that owneth this girdle, and shall deliver him into the hands of the Gentiles.

The New Testament prophet will have revelations of future events. Agabus had a revelation of a worldwide event, and a revelation of events that would occur in Paul's life.

Acts 13:1-2 Now there were in the church that was at Antioch certain prophets and teachers...As they ministered to the Lord, and fasted, the Holy Ghost said, Separate me Barnabas and Saul for the work whereunto I have called them.

Prophets will confirm God's plan and work in the ministry of his people. The prophets in Antioch realized through the Spirit, that it was time for Barnabas and Paul to be sent off to the work they were called to do.

The Prophet's Scope of Operation

God seems to use prophets in different scopes based on the need and according to His will. The prophet's scope has to do with the area or topic he primarily addresses. The prophet's scope is related to where or to whom the prophet is assigned. The prophet may be assigned to a place or to a certain group of people.

The scope in which a prophet primarily operates relates to the assignment, not the capacity. For instance, Moses was assigned to Israel – that was his prophetic scope. But many, if not all, of Moses' prophecies, had worldwide significance and impact. Moses often had face to face interactions with God, unlike other prophets. As the prophet who received the law, his ministry served as a type of Christ. Thus, Moses' capacity had a global impact, but his scope was for a nation.

Local

The local prophet is assigned to a local church or church body to build and propel the vision of the church. In the church age, every prophet will operate in this scope in some capacity. He serves as a clarifying voice to rally God's people to do the work of ministry that must be done now in the church. The prophet who mainly operates in this scope will often be used by God to identify and confirm spiritual gifts and callings upon members in a local church (Acts 13:1-3; 1 Timothy 4:14). In addition, God will use them to support the ministerial leadership in fulfilling the vision of the church.

God especially uses the local church prophet to be a vocal weapon in the time of challenges and battles in the local church. The prophet's voice plunders the enemy when the local church is under attack. The prophet stifles the voice of backbiters, slanderers, and critics who are seeking to break down the church.

There were prophets in the local church at Antioch. Acts 13:1 states, *"now in the church at Antioch there were prophets and teachers"*. Judas and Silas operated as prophets from the church in Jerusalem; they were a voice of truth strengthening and clarifying the decisions made by the church council in Jerusalem (Acts 15:27-32).

Nationwide

Some prophets primarily receive revelations and utterances for the local church, but others will function more for a nation. The prophet who operates in a nationwide scope is especially burdened for the state of a nation. This prophet will know what God is doing in a nation at a given time. Subsequently, he often speaks to the people, leaders, and stakeholders of that nation. This prophet will see what God will do in a nation through key individuals and leaders. He will also see the actions of organizations, other nations, and worldwide events that will specifically impact the nation where he is assigned.

The scope of Elijah's ministry seemed to have been mainly to the people of Israel; revelations he received of other nations were concerning how they would affect Israel. Samuel the prophet ministered primarily to the people of Israel, and to the first kings of Israel. The prophets Jonah and Nahum were especially burdened for Nineveh, the capital city of Assyria (Jonah 1-4; Nahum 1:1). Other than Israel, Obadiah had a specific burden for Edom (Obadiah 1:1).

Regional

The regional prophet operates similarly as the prophet assigned to a nation. This prophet may speak to the nations in the region of the country where he is assigned. The regional prophet is often burdened with the entire geographical territory of his assignment. The regional prophet will primarily prophesy of events and to people in the given region including a group of nations, continent, or a geographical border.

Global

The prophet who operates on a global scope will receive multiple revelations of events and key shifts around the world. This prophet will especially reveal God's global acts on the world. Jeremiah was a *"prophet unto the nations"* (Jeremiah 1:5).

It should be said here that all prophets speak globally, regionally, nationally and locally to some extent. However, prophets often will receive more revelations in the scope that they have been given. Since God is moving around the world, even the prophet with a local assignment will speak words that have a global impact. Distinguishing the prophet's scope is not to limit, but to provide a greater understanding of the office. This is to explain why some prophets function primarily in certain areas than others, but does not limit the impact a prophet can have.

Differences with Old Testament Prophets and Prophets of Today

Primarily Reveal than Command

In the Old Testament, the people of Israel understood the will of God through the law and the prophets. Outside of the laws of Moses, the people primarily heard the voice of God through the prophets. Today, the believer is not dependent upon the prophet to hear from God. Rather, the function of the prophet today is to empower the church to do the works of the ministry by being spokesmen for God, and through revealing the unknown. Though prophets of today can give scriptural commands, they primarily function by revealing the unknown. The revelations of a prophet are only commanding when they are directly related to

Scripture. For life matters not directly addressed in Scripture, prophets primarily reveal not command.

When Agabus gave the revelation to Paul of the persecution to come in Jerusalem, he did not command Paul to go or not go to Jerusalem. Agabus gave the revelation in his role to strengthen Paul in the accomplishment of his ministry, but it was not a command for Paul not to go to Jerusalem. Since the New Testament prophet does not mediate God's voice to the saint, the believers are still primarily responsible to knowing the voice of God. Succinctly, believers should not look to prophets today to give commanding directions, but rather to confirm, correct, and empower them to do what God has commanded.

In this sense, the prophecy of Scripture comes with greater authority than the words of a prophet today. The commanding New Testament prophecies of Scripture are binding on today's believer. Furthermore, Scripture is infallible. The words and prophecies written by the New Testament apostles and authors are commands for us to follow. But, the prophet today can only give personal commands to believers when he is speaking the words of Scripture.

Does Not Add to Scripture

Revelations given to prophets today do not add to Scripture. God designated certain prophets who gave the Scriptures we have today. For example, Moses, Aaron, and Miriam were prophets. But only Moses was used to give the law, and to write the first five books of the Bible. Aaron and Miriam prophesied, and had revelations, but it was not for Scripture, but only to empower the ongoing work of the Lord taking place at that time.

Even so the revelations given by prophets today are not Scripture, but are for the enablement of God's people to do ministry in our time. On the foundation of the original apostles of Christ, the New Testament canon of Scripture is already closed; therefore, there are no prophets existing today that add to Scripture.

I Corinthian 14:29 - 32 Let the prophets speak two or three, and let the other judge. If any thing be revealed to another that sitteth by, let the first hold his peace. For ye may all prophesy one by one, that all may learn, and all may be comforted. And the spirits of the prophets are subject to the prophets.

Revelations given by prophets today should not be taken as infallible. All prophetic revelations should be evaluated. When clear that a prophecy is from God, embrace and act upon it.

The New Testament prophet is a preacher of the word and a seer. His preaching and revelations equip the church to do the work of God. In fact, the prophet stimulates believers and the church to walk with prophetic insight. While prophetic revelations today are not equal to scriptural commands, according to Scripture, we should act on proven revelations.

Live Agents of Empowerment

The prophet is a live agent of God's empowerment. The utterance and revelations given through the prophet either announces God's active working in the world or stirs God's people to fulfill God's work. The person in the office of the prophet is a partner with God in his working on the earth. Read through the prophets and you will see that they converse with

God over the things that He is doing in Israel, other nations, and in their lives. God speaks back to them and tells the prophets His plans in the world.

Therefore, the prophet remains in sacred communication with God. The prophet speaks as an agent of God's working in the earth. God executes His plan through the voice of the prophet. The prophet trumpets so that the people will move. The prophet warns so that people will fear. The prophet exhorts to stir the work of ministry. The prophet is live and in action with God's current work on the earth. God does what the prophet speaks since the prophet speaks what God is doing. God does nothing without revealing it to a prophet (Amos 3:7).

> THE PROPHET IS LIVE AND IN ACTION WITH GOD'S CURRENT WORK ON THE EARTH.

Thus, God uses the office of the prophet to propel revival on the earth. Through their example and utterance, the prophets are leaders in sparking the prophetic revolution. God took the anointing on Moses and poured it upon seventy leaders. Two of the leaders were not at the gathering place and began to prophesy, but Joshua wanted to stop them. Wishing that all God's people would be prophets, Moses told Joshua not to be envious. Woe to the prophets who are jealous over the prophetic outpouring upon the everyday believer. Being partners with God, prophets must become instruments who impart the gift of prophecy and speak like Moses: *"would God that all the LORD'S people were prophets, and that the LORD would put his spirit upon them!"* (Numbers 11:29).

The Prophet's Work for the Prophetic Revolution

Below is a brief outline of the work of the person in the prophet's ministry office for the prophetic revolution.

1. To mobilize the body of Christ to the ministry by prophesying of their calling and purpose (Ephesians 4:11-12).

2. To impart spiritual gifts through prophesying. Prophets can prophesy the call and gifting that God reveals in a person's life (Acts 13:1-4; 1 Timothy 4:14).

3. To mentor and train the body of Christ in the prophetic. This would be like how Samuel, Elijah, and Elisha trained and mentored the sons of the prophets. Samuel led a company of them (1 Samuel 19:20); Elijah had a group that followed and observed him (2 Kings 2); Elisha had a group that stayed together with him for training. The Bible records how some of these sons of the prophets prophesied, and were given assignments by the leading prophet (2 Kings 9:1-2).

4. To guard the prophetic movement in the church by identifying and prophesying against false prophets (1 Kings 22:13-23; 1 Corinthians 14:29; Ezekiel 13:1-15).

5. Foster a prophetic environment in the local church, so that the Spirit of Prophecy can flow with the manifestation of prophetic utterances and revelations (1 Corinthians 12:27-28; Numbers 11:25-29; 1 Chronicles 25:1; 1 Corinthians 14:23-31).

6. Identify and trigger seasons and places of revival by prophesying to men and women whom God will use in those revivals (1 Kings 19:15-18).

7. Keep the church alert to the last day dangers prophesied in the Bible concerning the state of the church (Revelation 2:29).

In the prophetic revolution, God is stirring leading prophets to mobilize all believers to manifest the gift of prophecy in church ministry and evangelism.

11

BECOMING A PROPHETIC CHURCH

IN AN INCREASINGLY dark world void of the voice of truth, every church should cultivate the prophetic. The church is the prophetic voice of correction, warning, and truth to the world. Moreover, God will warn the church of impending calamities to come. The first-century Jerusalem church knew before of a coming famine because of prophetic revelation from the prophet Agabus. They had foreknowledge of the fall of the temple in Jerusalem due to the prophecy of Christ. The first-century Christian church was prophetic. For example, prophecy was active in the church at Corinth. The four daughters of the evangelist Philipp were prophets.

The church had insight into the prophetic revelations of the Old Testament concerning God's purposes and plans for the church. And, in the epistles of Paul, Peter, Jude, and John, there are prophecies of the things to come. The early church was prophetic.

God intends for the church to continue to be prophetic, admonishing the society around us, and warning of calamities to come.

God has used the Harvest Army Church International prophetically to warn the world of impending calamities to come. Leaders and laypeople have given multiple prophetic utterances and revelations. For example, the damaging earthquake in Haiti in January of 2010 was prophesied[xii]. In November of 2012, a prophetic revelation was given of "Storms, Tornadoes and the like loom upon the East USA". In November of 2012, the Super Storm Sandy hit the East Coast and New York[xiii].

In a dramatic revelation, the Southern part of Southern America was seen stretched. In March of 2010, fulfilling the prophecy, a massive earthquake hits Chile, and other surrounding countries, moving Chile's capital by 10 feet and shifting other parts of South America. News of the shifting was reported by CNN[xiv].

Moreover, every local church needs prophetic unction in their congregation for the health of the church. Before proceeding to the steps a church can take to cultivate a prophetic atmosphere in their congregation, I will first list some of the reasons why the prophetic is needed.

Why Churches Need to Become Prophetic

Prophecy benefits the church. Prophecy ignites, overthrows, encourages, comforts, sustains, corrects, and identifies.

Ignites the Saints to Work

Ezra 5:1-2 Then the prophets, Haggai the prophet, and Zechariah the son of Iddo, prophesied unto the Jews that were in Judah and Jerusalem in the name of the God of Israel, even unto them. Then rose up Zerubbabel the son of Shealtiel, and Jeshua the son of Jozadak, and began to build the house of God which is at Jerusalem: and with them were the prophets of God helping them.

The rebuilding of the temple had ceased due to different obstacles from the enemies of Judah. It was the prophecies of Haggai and Zechariah that stirred the leaders and people to continue the rebuilding of the temple. The people were stirred up to work through the prophetic utterances and revelations from the prophets. Furthermore, the prophets helped through the reconstruction by providing prophetic insight for the furtherance of the work.

The prophetic unction in a local congregation is necessary to stir people out of complacency and move them to fulfill the vision of the church. Church members can even discover and confirm their ministries and gifting through prophetic ministry (Acts 13:1-4; I Timothy 4:14). Prophecy ignites God's people to do the work of the ministry.

Overthrows the Enemies Plans

Imagine gathering in your local church on Sunday morning, and then having to run for cover as bullets shoot around the sanctuary. In November of 2017, using a military-style rifle, a man shot and killed 26 congregants of a small Baptist church in the rural town of Sutherland Springs, Texas. Another 20 people were injured. It was only a few minutes after 11 am at the start of the Sunday morning worship service. Among the dead were children, women, and even the pastor's teenage daughter[xv].

With local churches facing unsuspected gun attacks like this, they need prophetic revelation from the Lord. Sure, church leaders, politicians, and other experts will recommend steps churches can take to protect their congregation. But a prophetic church can have what no human analysts can produce – revelation knowledge of impending danger.

Some local churches have been weakened and divided by the works of the devil through false accusations, slander, and divisions. Well-meaning church leaders and members try to intervene to solve the problem before the church is severely weakened but to no avail. Prophetic utterance and revelation can accomplish what church meetings, attempts at reconciliation, and counseling alone cannot do. Local churches need prophecy to counteract the divisive and destructive works of evil working against them.

Misdirects the enemy

When Saul, King of Israel, sent messengers to capture David, God used a company of prophets to deter the messengers from reaching David. The Spirit of Prophecy came upon the messengers, and instead of apprehending David, they were found prophesying among the prophets. This happened at least three times as Saul continued to send messengers to arrest David. Finally, Saul went himself, but he was found prophesying also when he came among the company of prophets. Thus, God used the prophetic unction to prevent David from being captured by Saul.

> *1 Samuel 19:20-24 And Saul sent messengers to take David: and when they saw the company of the prophets prophesying, and Samuel standing as*

appointed over them, the Spirit of God was upon the messengers of Saul, and they also prophesied. And when it was told Saul, he sent other messengers, and they prophesied likewise. And Saul sent messengers again the third time, and they prophesied also. Then went he also to Ramah, and came to a great well that is in Sechu: and he asked and said, Where are Samuel and David? And one said, Behold, they be at Naioth in Ramah. And he went thither to Naioth in Ramah: and the Spirit of God was upon him also, and he went on, and prophesied, until he came to Naioth in Ramah. And he stripped off his clothes also, and prophesied before Samuel in like manner, and lay down naked all that day and all that night. Wherefore they say, Is Saul also among the prophets?

When the Spirit of Prophecy is operating in a local assembly, often God will misdirect the works of troublemakers (slanderers, dividers, accusers, etc.). I have witnessed troublemakers trying to bring division in a local church by spreading lies to their friends and confidants who are also members of the same church. But instead, God will give prophetic revelations to the same members being targeted, revealing the wrong intentions of the troublemakers. As a result, the very members, the troublemakers thought were on their side, report their evil deeds to the leaders of the congregation.

Exposes the enemy

2 Kings 6:12 And one of his servants said, None, my lord, O king: but Elisha, the prophet that is in Israel, telleth the king of Israel the words that thou speakest in thy bedchamber.

Elisha the prophet was informing the King of Israel of the location of Syria's next attack. Realizing Israel's readiness for all his attacks, the King of Syria suspected that there was a spy among his people. However, it was the prophet receiving the revelation of their plans.

God will reveal the works of evil to local church leaders and workers who are expecting to hear from God. God may expose divisive actions and intentions in detail. Alternatively, God may lead church leaders in an unsuspecting way to counteract the plans of the devil.

The Harvest Army World Revival Movement released a prophecy on March 14, 2019 that exposes the plans of the enemy against ministries that broadcast online. The following is the prophecy:

> *In a vision, it seems like ministers from different churches discover that there is benefit from doing ministry at a certain spot in front of some high poles or the like. After a few had done it security officials intervened and dismantled their efforts. Interpretation: Christian ministries will experience major restriction and removal from internet platforms shortly.*

God has given the above revelation so that ministries can make steps against the plans of internet platforms to restrict Christian ministries. God will expose the plans of the devil against churches and ministries.

Challenges the enemy

At times, a local church must make an open stand against the works of evil that is operating in the local community, or the global society. Through prophecy, the church can take a bold demonstrative stand against evil.

The prophet Elijah, under the prophetic unction, challenged the four hundred (400) prophets of Baal. He prophetically declared "*the God that answereth by fire let him be God*" (I Kings 18:24). Of course, only the God of Israel answered by fire. This was a clear prophetic demonstration of God's Sovereignty. When the church prophesies boldly and accurately, it demonstrates the power of God. Instead of kowtowing to political correctness and societal trends, the church must call the society to repentance, and warn of impending judgment with prophetic authority. The local church that gives in to the evil trends in society will become irrelevant and lose its influence in the world.

Encourages the Leaders

Judges 5:12 Awake, awake, Deborah: awake, awake, utter a song: arise, Barak, and lead thy captivity captive, thou son of Abinoam.

Through the prophecy of the prophet Deborah, Barak, the leader of the army, received courage to lead the Israeli military to victory. God will use prophetic utterance and revelations to encourage a leader to act on God's plan.

Comforts the Saints

1 Corinthians 14:3 But he that prophesieth speaketh unto men to edification, and exhortation, and comfort.

God uses prophetic utterances to comfort and encourage the saints to remain faithful and to do the work of the ministry.

Sustains the Work

Ezra 6:14 And the elders of the Jews builded, and they prospered through the prophesying of Haggai the prophet and Zechariah the son of Iddo. And they builded, and finished it,

Without the prophecies of Haggai and Zechariah, it's doubtful the Jewish leaders would have continued well in the rebuilding of the temple. They prospered and completed the work through prophecy. Even so, God's people are stirred to continue and complete the work of the kingdom to accomplish the vision of the church through prophetic utterance and revelation.

Corrects Wrong

God often uses prophets to correct wrongdoing. The prophet Nathan corrected David of his immoral and murderous actions in 2 Samuel 12:1-13. Samuel the prophet corrected Saul of his disobedience to God's command (1 Samuel 15:22-23). Moreover, God sent various prophets to correct Israel from its rebellion (2 Chronicles 36:15-16).

God will use prophetic utterance to admonish the church and to rebuke immoral activity. The Lord will give prophetic revelations to reveal wrongdoing and evil intentions that are taking place. The holy fear of God can come upon a church as God supernaturally reveals ungodly acts spurring repentance and spiritual renewal.

Identifies God's Next Move

When Elijah was burned out and thought he was alone, God revealed to him the next set of leaders that he should anoint to complete the work (I Kings 19:14-18). Prophecy can reignite churches that seem to be plateauing and becoming complacent. God will use prophetic revelations to identify and confirm strategic next steps in the visionary development and growth of a church. This includes new leaders that should be appointed and commissioned.

> *Acts 13:1-3 Now there were in the church that was at Antioch certain prophets and teachers; as Barnabas, and Simeon that was called Niger, and Lucius of Cyrene, and Manaen, which had been brought up with Herod the tetrarch, and Saul. As they ministered to the Lord, and fasted, the Holy Ghost said, Separate me Barnabas and Saul for the work whereunto I have called them. And when they had fasted and prayed, and laid their hands on them, they sent them away.*

In addition, God will reveal the right time to commission a new ministry or mission within the development of a church. While prophets and other church leaders in Antioch were praying, God revealed that it was time for Paul and Barnabas to be released into the next phase of ministry.

How to Become a Prophetic Church

Mobilize the Pew to Preach the Gospel

The local church that is consistently engaged in winning the lost through gospel preaching and personal evangelism are ready to receive from the Spirit of Prophecy. Remember that it is the Spirit of Prophecy that moved the Old Testament prophets to speak of Christ to come. Through the same Spirit, the gospel is preached today. The testimony of Jesus is the Spirit of Prophecy. Churches where the members consistently proclaim the gospel and Christ's soon return operate under the Spirit of Prophecy; therefore, the evangelistic church is fertile ground for prophetic insight.

Pastors and church leaders should activate their congregation to regularly preach and witness on the streets and from house to house in their city. It may begin by simply handing out gospel tracts, and quoting John 3:16 aloud on the streets. Additionally, it may involve personal, one-to-one sharing of the gospel, house to house evangelism, preaching on public transport vehicles, and other variety of methods.

Prophesy the Word of God

The Bible is prophetic. Pastors and church leaders that prophetically expound on the Word of God are training their congregation to have prophetic insight. There are several ways pastors and church leaders can prophesy using the Word of God.

1. Use the Bible to prophesy on societal and governmental Sins.

    a. Give prophetic insight on the reasons for the current conditions of the society, and the promised hope if people turn to God.

    b. Warn against immorality and prophesy of its consequences.

    c. Warn against societal and governmental oppression and injustices and warn of its dire consequences.

2. Prophesy Future Prophecies of Scripture

    a. Speak about the prophecies of Scripture concerning the last days.

      b. Speak about the prophecies of the state of society just before Christ returns.

      c. Give the prophecies about the judgment to come, the judgment of each person, the coming millennium, and the new heaven and new earth.

3. Train the congregation to recognize and share with others the calamities and behaviors happening today that were clearly prophesied in Scripture.

Partner with A Prophet/Prophetic Church

1 Samuel 10:10 And when they came thither to the hill, behold, a company of prophets met him; and the Spirit of God came upon him, and he prophesied among them

The prophetic anointing is transferable. In the Old Testament, the Spirit of Prophecy would come upon those who would join a company of prophets. God took the spirit that was upon Moses and placed it upon seventy elders, and they all prophesied. The apostle Paul laid hands upon believers in Ephesus, and they prophesied.

Therefore, a church can begin to operate in the prophetic by partnering with a prophetic ministry or church. Allow a proven, godly living prophet to minister to the congregation. Be careful to ensure that the prophet is one that is proven by the accurate fulfillment of multiple prophecies and evidence of a godly living lifestyle. The person does not need to have the title "prophet." Rather, receive any godly living minister of the gospel who faithfully preaches the Word of God and often operates in the gift of prophecy and prophetic revelation with accurate fulfillment. Furthermore, fellowship with churches that demonstrate evidence of the prophetic manifesting in their midst.

When you partner with a prophetic ministry or church, highlight the prophecies and fulfillments that are given by true prophets. Take the time to publicly speak prophecies that are provided by a proven prophetic ministry or church. Then highlight the fulfillment of the prophecy when it occurs.

Minister the Baptism of the Spirit

Some assemblies no longer emphasize or encourage the baptism of the Spirit with the evidence of speaking in tongues. However, there is a direct correlation between the outpouring of the Spirit and the prophetic revolution. God promises the Spirit's outpouring in the last days, which is now. The outpouring of the Spirit upon the church brings the unction to prophesy as spoken of in Joel 2:28. Prophetic utterance is sure evidence of the baptism of the Holy Spirit.

When a person receives Christ, the Holy Spirit indwells them, bringing spiritual regeneration. Subsequently, the same Spirit within the believer overflows and comes upon the believer empowering him for spiritual service; this is the baptism of the Spirit. It is this coming upon by the Spirit that brings prophetic utterance.

Since the prophetic unction is needed in our time to stand in the society, churches must stress the importance of the baptism of the Holy Spirit. Pastors and church leaders should teach all believers about the baptism of the Spirit and take the time to minister to believers to receive this gift from the Lord.

Encourage Members to Seek for the Gift of Prophecy

1 Corinthians 14:1 Follow after charity, and desire spiritual gifts, but rather that ye may prophesy

Church leaders should teach the importance of the gift of prophecy, and the scriptural instruction to desire and seek for its manifestation. This is a direct teaching from the Bible.

The Bible instructs explicitly to pray for prophetic utterance. Paul taught that when there is a public manifestation of the gift of tongues that the church should pray for the interpretation. Interpretation of tongues is equal to the gift of prophecy(1 Corinthians 14:5). Furthermore, Paul taught to covet to prophesy from which we can conclude that we should pray for the manifestation of the gift of prophecy in the church.

Expect Prophetic Utterance

While praying for the manifestation of the gift of prophecy, there should be an expectation of faith that prophetic utterances and revelations will begin to manifest in the church. Encourage members to prophesy and acknowledge when a prophecy is from the Lord.

Encourage the people to write down revelations, dreams, visions, word of knowledge, etc. that they receive from the Lord and share it with the pastoral team. Publicly speak those prophetic revelations that have been tested and are clearly from the Lord.

Maintain Order

As the faith of a church begins to rise in expectation of the manifestation of prophecy, prophetic utterance and revelation will take place. Several members in the church may begin to speak aloud in prophetic utterance in the church, and more will present their prophetic revelations. While this is happening, the ministerial leaders of the church must diligently endeavor to maintain order while not quenching the prophetic fervor in the congregation.

During worship services, depending on the size and composition of the church, generally, one person speaks at a time while someone records to evaluate and republish the prophecy. All others should listen and assess the prophetic utterance. Two or three may speak at the same time if this can happen without confusion, and a group of witnesses can hear each one. Again, someone should be designated to record the utterances of each person so that it can be further evaluated and possibly republished. Huge churches may need to train ministerial teams to listen to and record prophecies in the congregation at appropriate times. Otherwise, the utterer can privately share the message with a ministerial leader without disrupting the order of service. The goal is to encourage the manifestation of the gift while maintaining order.

Prophetic revelations, dreams, and visions, those that are meant for the public, from lay prophets in the church should first be evaluated by ministerial leaders, or an appointed team before publicized or acted upon. Pastoral leaders should ensure that revelations that are spoken to the church or acted upon have been vetted for accuracy.

Develop A Process for Judging Revelations

Implement a process of discerning and interpreting dreams and revelations based upon the following biblical principles.

1. Do not despise prophecies. Encourage leaders and congregants to share their prophetic utterances and revelations, including dreams, visions, word of knowledge, etc. While testing all things, do not quench the gift.

2. Reject anything that undermines the deity and humanity of Christ. Any form of revelation that denies, even in part, that Jesus Christ is fully God and fully man should be rejected.

3. Reject anything unbiblical and carnal.

4. Create a team of those gifted in interpretation, discernment, and prophecy who will judge prophecies and revelations that are given.

5. The team should prayerfully look over and evaluate revelations.

6. Evaluate the life and character of the person giving the revelation or prophecy.

    a. Are they committed to the local church and its leadership?

- b. Have they demonstrated fruits of godly living or repentance?
- c. Are their teachings and doctrines biblical?
- d. Have they previously given a prophecy or revelation that came to pass?

7. Evaluate the credibility and necessity of the prophecy or revelation.
    - a. Is it biblically aligned? Reject anything that violates any command or teaching of Scripture.
    - b. Are there any confirmations, leading, or prompting from the Spirit that it is from God?
    - c. What impact will it have? For example, will it build up or destroy a church? A "revelation" that would be destructive or divisive may not be from God. However, some revelations may be from God but should not be released publicly but handled discretely.
    - d. What is the purpose? The purpose may be to bring warning, to edify, to comfort, to correct, to glorify God, to confirm, to ignite, to mobilize, etc. When unable to determine a purpose, it may be best to rest the revelation until receiving further clarity.

8. Only publish prophecies and revelations that are proven and sure. A prophecy may be from God, but if the team is unsure, keep it unpublished and ask the Lord to give further clarity. God will often reveal the matter in a

different way or through someone else. The responsibility of the church is to apply the command of Scripture to evaluate the prophecy.

Recognize Proven Prophets in the Church

Developing the prophetic unction in a local church will open the door for the Lord to appoint some members to the office of a prophet. The pastoral leadership should recognize the prophetic office on faithful leaders and members who consistently prophesy with accurate fulfillments and preach the truth.

Often God will confirm the ministry of the prophet in a local church by using him or her to give multiple strategic prophetic revelations and utterances for the development of the church. Or, the Lord may give the person numerous revelations concerning events in the nation or around the world with accurate fulfillments. Therefore, leaders will clearly see the need for the ministry of that prophet in the assembly.

The leaders can publicly acknowledge the gift in the person through a declaration, and a formal ordination. Local congregations may connect with a prophetic ministry for the public appointment of the person to the ministry office of prophet.

Exalt Jesus Christ Exclusively

Revelation 19:10 I fell at his feet to worship him. And he said unto me, See thou do it not: I am thy fellowservant, and of thy brethren that have the testimony of Jesus: worship God: for the testimony of Jesus is the spirit of prophecy.

While you acknowledge proven prophets, the glory must remain on Christ. Fulfilled prophecies should be publicly acknowledged so that God is glorified in all things. Strictly avoid the exaltation of any man who is mightily used by God in prophecy. Exaltation of a prophet will kill the prophetic unction. As the prophet is only a representative for God, his message should only give glory to God.

The prophetic revelations and utterances are from the Lord through the Holy Spirit. We are only his servants. Ensure that all praise goes to Him. And every person who receives many prophetic revelations should diligently maintain a humble spirit (2 Corinthians 12:7-10).

Guard Against False Prophecy

Avoid giving space to anyone who claims to be a prophet but is unproven in character and reputation.

Avoid giving space to any type of claimed prophecy or revelation that engineers rebellion and slander of local church leaders, and fuels backbiting and gossiping.

Give no room to the spirit of divination. The spirit of divination acts as a counterfeit form of prophecy. Any form of revelation that comes through consulting the dead, palm reading, psychic readings, horoscopes, astrology, etc. are from the devil. Some churches invite the spirit of divination through incense burning, Old Testament ritualism, and unbiblical sacraments.

Jeremiah 23:28 The prophet that hath a dream, let him tell a dream; and he that hath my word, let him speak my word faithfully. What is the chaff to the wheat? saith the LORD

More can be read about guarding against false prophecy in the next chapter, chapter 12.

The Process at Harvest Army Church International

Since the late twentieth century, the Harvest Army Church has been prophesying of events to come upon the earth. However, from 2004 with the ninth (9th) hour revelation, a multiplied number of prophecies have been given through the ministry. Leaders and members of the church alike have given many prophetic revelations over the years that all came to pass. The Chief Presiding Bishop of the church body often states that the main actions of the church are fasting and praying, preaching the gospel, and living a holy life. The following is the process that the church follows to evaluate and publish prophetic utterances and revelations.

Encouragement of members to operate in the gift. All members and even friends of the ministry are encouraged to submit prophetic utterances and revelations, including dreams, visions, etc.

A team is appointed to evaluate. A selected team of mature and proven workers has access to read over and check the prophecies and revelations.

The team evaluates the lay prophets' prophecies. The selected team members assess the prophecies and decide if they are from God or not. This decision is made based on the known character, and the reputation of the person submitting the prophecy. The person's character is evaluated based on the person's integrity, manner of life, commitment to a local church body, and accountability to local church leadership. Evaluation of the person's reputation has to do with the accuracy of past prophetic utterances and revelations given by the person, and whether the person's teachings and doctrines are biblically sound. In the case where a person may be a new or unknown believer, the leaders or team will seek for a confirmation from the Spirit of God.

Each utterance or revelation is scrutinized. Finally, even with a proven reputation, we determine if each submitted utterance or revelation is from God. If we are unsure, we leave the prophecy alone and wait for further revelation from God. Our decision is based on biblical alignment, the witness of the Spirit, and whether the given utterance or revelation has any purpose. For example, we often reject predictions of the identity of the next United States' president during the election season since such prophecies have little to no spiritual edification and rarely glorifies God.

Interpretation of the prophecy as needed. Often, we ask the lay prophet to state their interpretation of the revelation. Secondly, those with the gift to interpret dreams and visions will give their insight. Interpretation is made prayerfully. God must supernaturally provide the interpretation of a dream or revelation; it is not determined by natural or rational analysis.

Publication. The revelations and prophecies are publicly spoken often in groups of three. The prophecy is also publicly released in written form online. Only prophecies and revelations that are sure will be distributed. Doubtful revelations and prophecies are not published even if it may be from God. Remaining faithful in evaluating every revelation, if a true prophecy is not published, we believe God will provide greater clarity or reveal it differently.

Prophecy Summits. We provide an opportunity for training and guidance in prophetic revelations through periodic prophecy summits. During this event, a panel of leaders answer questions from the audience about dreams, visions, and other prophetic revelations. The leaders will give insight into determining if the revelations are from the Lord, and on how to interpret them. The Bible is used as the foundational source for answering questions from the audience. We are diligent in ensuring that revelations with sensitive information is not publicly shared. Some answers are given privately or at a later time as needed.

The process at the Harvest Army Church International is based on the instructions of 1 Corinthians 14 along with the general biblical understanding of God's working in revelations. Every church looking to be prophetic will need to develop a similar process based on God's word to ensure order.

Prophetic churches are training grounds to mobilize the people of God for the prophetic revolution. New prophetic voices will continue to arise out of faithful prophetic churches that adhere to Scripture and follows the Spirit. Pastors can foster a prophetic environment within their church by encouraging their members to desire the gift and by practicing the other principles in this chapter.

12

GUARDING AGAINST FALSE PROPHECY

Ezekiel 13:2-7 Son of man, prophesy against the prophets of Israel that prophesy, and say thou unto them that prophesy out of their own hearts, Hear ye the word of the LORD; Thus saith the Lord GOD; Woe unto the foolish prophets, that follow their own spirit, and have seen nothing! O Israel, thy prophets are like the foxes in the deserts. Ye have not gone up into the gaps, neither made up the hedge for the house of Israel to stand in the battle in the day of the LORD. They have seen vanity and lying divination, saying, The LORD saith: and the LORD hath not sent them: and they have made others to hope that they would confirm the word. Have ye not seen a vain vision, and have ye not spoken a lying divination, whereas ye say, The LORD saith it; albeit I have not spoken?

A PROPHETIC REVOLUTION is taking place. During this explosion of prophetic manifestation, the devil will bring counterfeits to undermine the prophetic voice and confuse the people of God. However, the Bible gives us the characteristics of false prophecy. Every believer and church should be aware of the signs of false prophecy with readiness to discern the difference between true and false prophecy.

There was a lady who often mistrusted her husband and was jealous over the slightest interaction he had with other females. To tell this story, I will call her Jolissa. Jolissa eventually shared with me that she believed some ladies in a certain church were trying to seduce her husband. A friend of hers, another Christian who supposedly receives revelations from God, had a dream in which some of the ladies in a church wanted to seduce Jolissa's husband. The ladies in the dream were committed Christians and faithful workers in their local church. I quickly told Jolissa that the dream was not from God and that it was devilish. Although Jolissa was warned not to believe the dream, she allowed her emotions to direct her. As a result, she created conflicts within the church and sowed discord in her marriage by accusing her husband and others of things that they did not do. The Christian who had the dream never corrected the wrong. And Jolissa regretted the outcome of her actions since it almost completely ruined her marriage. We cannot believe every revelation that we hear (1 John 4:1).

So how did I know that the dream was devilish? First, the dream was an accusation. The dream did not "reveal" that adultery was taking place, but rather that there was a desire to seduce. This is an accusation that cannot be corroborated with any evidence. Secondly, the dream was vilifying committed workers in a church, and confirming the carnal emotions of Jolissa. It would only sow discord between the sister and other members of the church. Any so-called "revelation" that accuse the righteous, and strengthen carnality is false. Furthermore, dreams and utterances that sow discord and divide a church are diabolical. True revelations edify the church and stir the righteous.

Now, let us see from the Bible how we can identify false prophecies, and guard ourselves against giving false prophecies and revelations. First, what is the nature of false prophecy?

False prophecy comes from the heart of men instead of the Spirit of God. They are often based on fleshly desires, emotions, and self-will. Describing false prophets, Ezekiel the prophet declares, "...*prophesy against the prophets of Israel that prophesy, and say thou unto them that prophesy out of their own hearts...Woe unto the foolish prophets, that follow their own spirit, and have seen nothing!*" People can have dreams, visions, and hear voices that are a product of their own desires, emotions, and self-determination (Jeremiah 14:14; 23:16). But it is not God. Humans can imagine visions and stir their own dreams by their personal desires, conclusions, and determinations. However, our desires, conclusions, and our passions can be opposite to those of the will of God.

False prophecy will always fail to support and build the local church. Prophets and prophetic declarations that abandon biblically-based local churches, especially in time of need, are false. False prophets will stand with slanderers and dividers of a local church, and forsake the church in its day of attack, trouble, and challenges. The true prophet will hold up the walls of the church in the day of trouble. Ezekiel 13:4-5 says, "*thy prophets are like the foxes in the deserts*" (KJV). "*You have not gone up into the breaches, or built up a wall for the house of Israel, that it might stand in battle in the day of the LORD*" (ESV). True prophecy will fortify local churches in times of an attack and prepare them for the day of battle.

Back to the story of Jolissa, she sought to confirm the false dream by looking for any accusable interaction between her husband and other ladies. She would accuse her husband of infidelity from just a stare, an eye contact, or a cordial greeting. When she observed these harmless interactions, she would point to them as confirmation of the accusatory dream. False prophets produce a dream from their own heart and then wish for its confirmation. God will always fulfill His word. However, the message of a false prophecy can seem to be confirmable, even though it is not the Lord that fulfilled it. Humans, through their own actions, can seek to produce something they imagined. Furthermore, there is always the chance that something spoken may happen. The power of true prophecy is that the Lord will fulfill what He has spoken, and that He is all-knowing. Unlike the words of psychics, true prophecy is not wishing for the thing to happen to have veracity. Rather, the power of real prophecy is that it's from the Lord.

Finally, false prophecies comfort the rebellious and hurts the righteous. Addressing the false prophets, God described the results of their lies saying, *"to slay the souls that should not die, and to save the souls alive that should not live, by your lying to my people that hear your lies?" (Ezekiel 13:19)*. Where the door is given, the words of false prophets will often damage or hinder the work of God. False prophets or prophecies can be recognized in a local church, when the prophecies generate strife, division, and hamper the work of the church. True prophecies will always edify and strengthen the faithful workers in a church as well as the church body. Any prophecy that seeks to bring down a local biblical church is false. Moreover, deceitful prophecies malign godly church leaders and faithful workers.

False prophets use ungodly means of conjuring up revelations. Due to the increasing manifestations of the gift of prophecy, there are counterfeit manifestations also on the rise. There are a small minority of churches that as of this writing are even employing psychic mediums on their ministerial staff[xvi]. Surely, any utterance or prediction that comes from consulting the dead, horoscopes, psychic connections, African spiritism, palm reading, astrology, tarot card readings, voodoo, witchcraft, and Wiccan practices are of the devil. True prophecy is first the prophecies of the Bible; additionally, only prophecies that come from the Spirit of God. God-given prophecies occur as the Spirit moves the believer, not through external objects and concoctions.

How to Guard Against False Prophecy

Stick with Scripture

2 Peter 1:19 We have also a more sure word of prophecy; whereunto ye do well that ye take heed, as unto a light that shineth in a dark place…

Jeremiah 23:28 The prophet that hath a dream, let him tell a dream; and he that hath my word, let him speak my word faithfully. What is the chaff to the wheat? saith the LORD.

No current revelation or utterance can superimpose Scripture. Every prophetic utterance and revelation should be evaluated using the Bible. If a prophecy violates the teaching of Scripture, it should be discarded. Every believer can use the Scriptures to assess revelations that he receives to see if they are from God. Every prophecy is weighed by Scripture. If a prophecy is found contradicting the Scriptures in any way, it is not from God.

Furthermore, believers must reject any person claiming to be in the prophetic office but are unscriptural in their teachings. Even if the words of a prophet seem to be fulfilled, if the prophet teaches doctrine that contradicts the gospel of Christ, and the clear teachings of Scripture, he should be rejected.

Confirm the Word with Prophetic Witnesses

1 Corinthians 14:29 Let the prophets speak two or three, and let the other judge.

God confirms matters through two or three witnesses (Matthew 18:16; 2 Corinthians 13:1). Usually, God will reveal His will to at least two or three others to confirm His word. He may confirm a prophecy by giving you assurance or a similar message. Secondly, others will provide similar prophetic revelations and utterances to confirm the word.

Dismiss Questionable Revelations

Be willing to discard any revelation that seems dubious. Perhaps there are no confirming witnesses, or you sense discomfort with a prophecy that is given. It may seem to contradict other revelations given to you or others from the Lord. Since God commands us to prove all prophecies, it is scriptural to ignore doubtful prophecies. If it is the Lord, God knows how to get our attention so that we understand that He is speaking.

Unfollow Prophets with Unfulfilled Prophecies

Deuteronomy 18:22 When a prophet speaketh in the name of the LORD, if the thing follow not, nor come to pass, that is the thing which the LORD hath not spoken, but the prophet hath spoken it presumptuously: thou shalt not be afraid of him.

Since the gift of prophecy is being poured out on a massive scale some believers may need correction and teaching to operate maturely in the gift. Given human weakness, some believers can make mistakes. Therefore, all prophecies should be tested. Discard unscriptural, unconfirmed, and dubious prophecies.

However, those who claim to be in the office of the prophet carry a greater responsibility. Believers have a responsibility to unfollow prophets with multiple prophecies that fail to come to pass. Avoid prophets who lack accountable leadership. Additionally, stay away from prophets who exchange personal prophecies for monetary reward, and claim to prophesy on demand. The office of the prophet is a sacred call. The so-called prophet who gives prophecies that do not come to pass discredits God.

Reject Divination

Deuteronomy 18:10-11 There shall not be found among you any one that maketh his son or his daughter to pass through the fire, or that useth divination, or an observer of times, or an enchanter, or a witch, Or a charmer, or a consulter with familiar spirits, or a wizard, or a necromancer.

Divination is an unbiblical attempt to receive supernatural revelations; consulting the spirit world, outside of Christ, using earthly objects and methods. This includes astrology, consulting the dead, horoscope, palm-reading, tarot card reading, voodoo, African spiritism, witchcraft, Wiccan practices, and other similar activities. God does not speak in any of these fashions. Rather they are demonic.

Reject Date-Setters of the Rapture or Christ's Return

Mark 13:32 But of that day and that hour knoweth no man, no, not the angels which are in heaven, neither the Son, but the Father.

Acts 1:7-8 And he said unto them, It is not for you to know the times or the seasons, which the Father hath put in his own power.

Predicting the date of the rapture of the church or the second return of Christ disregards the plain teaching of Scripture. To their detriment, some believers have erroneously followed leaders who predicted the date Christ would return, by even selling their houses and properties.

God the Father will not give prophecies of the date and hour for Christ's return; He has kept this knowledge for Himself. Eagerly, the gift of prophecy is given to fire up the church for ministry and to bring convincing evidence of the gospel. Therefore, the church must focus on keeping the fire until the coming of the Lord and avoid setting apocalyptic dates.

Reject Prophecies Based on Old Testament Ritualism

Colossians 2:16-17 Let no man therefore judge you in meat, or in drink, or in respect of an holyday, or of the new moon, or of the sabbath days: Which are a shadow of things to come; but the body is of Christ.

Galatians 3:5 He therefore that ministereth to you the Spirit, and worketh miracles among you, doeth he it by the works of the law, or by the hearing of faith?

Galatians 4:9-10 But now, after that ye have known God, or rather are known of God, how turn ye again to the weak and beggarly elements, whereunto ye desire again to be in bondage? Ye observe days, and months, and times, and years.

Some have attempted to prophesy of coming events using the symbolism from Old Testament feasts and rituals. Many of these prophecies fail. Often their analysis sound very convincing. However, anything beyond the plain commands of Scripture will fail. The Bible teaches us to avoid getting caught up in Old Testament ritual days and feasts. The testimony of Jesus is the Spirit of Prophecy. Old Testament rituals and feasts were only a shadow of what Christ would accomplish. The shadow has passed and we have the true substance in Christ. While symbolism in Old Testament feasts and ceremonies may give insight into our blessings in Christ, we should not seek to predict the future through these means. Prophecy today will not come from the shadow, but through the revelations given by the Spirit in Christ Jesus.

Reject Prophecies from False Religions

Isaiah 41:23-24 Shew the things that are to come hereafter, that we may know that ye are gods: yea, do good, or do evil, that we may be dismayed, and behold it together. Behold, ye are of nothing, and your work of nought: an abomination is he that chooseth you.

There are a set of internet-based preachers and teachers who consult prophecies from non-Christian religions to prophesy or confirm prophecies. This is unscriptural. Any prediction from a non-Christian religion should be categorically rejected.

Some may ask, but what if the prophecy from a non-Christian religion is like a biblical prophecy? When Aaron, Moses' assistant, miraculously turned his rod into a snake before Pharaoh, Pharaoh had his magicians to do the same. However, the snake from Aaron's rod swallowed up the snakes from the magicians of Egypt (Exodus 7:8-12). Even though a prediction from a false religion may seem accurate, it cannot be compared with revelation from the One and True God. Predictions that originate from worshippers of idols are false. The gods of false religions cannot predict accurately. Any seeming accuracy is only by chance, not from true revelation.

Embrace True Revelations

1 Thessalonians 5:20-21 Despise not prophesyings. Prove all things; hold fast that which is good.

First, embrace biblical prophecies. Knowledge of the Word of God and the prophecies of Scripture provide the strongest guard against false prophecy. Secondly, when the gift of prophecy truly manifests, believers should embrace the gift. As we practice to reject unscriptural and dubious prophecies and embrace genuine prophecies our senses become more attuned to recognizing an accurate word from the Lord.

13

THE EYEWITNESSES

THE FIRST APOSTLES of Christ were eyewitnesses of His glory and resurrection. The apostle Peter witnessed as Jesus was transfigured before him, and three other disciples in the mountain. He was also a witness of Christ after He rose again. Therefore, the apostles did not need to formulate false stories, and charismatic speeches in their declaration of the gospel, but gave firsthand testimony of His glory.

The first Apostles saw Jesus in His resurrected body. However, Anna and Simeon, spoken of at the beginning of Luke's gospel, recognized Christ as the Messiah from the time that he was a baby. They were eyewitnesses of fulfilled prophecy, and through prophetic insight were witnesses of Christ's glory even while he was a baby. Through the Spirit, Anna and Simeon had the prophetic insight to recognize the fulfillment of Messianic prophecy.

Today, God has eyewitnesses around the world. They evangelize with power and conviction because, through the Spirit, they can "see" the unveiling of prophecy in our time. The eyewitnesses are men, women, boys and girls around the world who cannot be silenced by compromise, threat, social pressure, or persecution because they are "seeing" the prophetic hands of God. They not only read about Jesus, and exegete text, but they hear his voice - walking and talking with him daily. They have clarity concerning God's prophetic plan because they "see" it by the Spirit. They can discern the difference between good and evil because they have exercised themselves in applying the Word of God to all things. They recognize the fulfillment of prophecy and being aware of the signs of the times, speak boldly that Jesus Christ is coming back soon.

> They not only read about Jesus, and exegete text, but they hear his voice.

A growing separation is developing between those who only have theological knowledge and those with the conviction of being eyewitnesses. The gap widens between those conducting ministry in human wisdom and those who know their God. It includes the religious elite versus the nobodies who are seeing the Lord.

The eyewitnesses have the conviction of "seeing" the Lord in action. While the scholars of liberal seminaries doubt supernatural spiritual gifts, and regulate them to the past, God's remnant of "seers" are witnessing the unfolding of prophecy today and hearing from the Lord. Clearly, these are not eyewitnesses who have seen Jesus in the flesh. But I speak of those who have "seen" the Lord as described in the next few paragraphs.

They Have Experienced Prophetic Fulfillment

Through Revelation in Their Own Lives

The eyewitnesses have heard the voice of God. Consistently, they see the things that God has spoken to them being fulfilled in their daily living. Because they know the voice of God, their lives have been ordered; and recognizing God's hand, they carry the conviction of knowing God. As it states in Daniel 11:32 *but the people that do know their God shall be strong, and do exploits.* They boldly do the things of God because they consistently hear the voice of God and are led by his Spirit.

All believers can be eyewitnesses since John 10:27 says, *my sheep hear my voice, and I know them, and they follow me.* Christians must go beyond only hearing and reading about prophecy, and experience the prophetic in their lives as they hear the voice of God and follow him. Believers who have a growing relationship with the Lord will know His voice and become witnesses of His prophetic hand. The eyewitnesses know God's voice and reject false teachings and prophecies. They discern fables and myths because of their devotion to the Lord.

Jeremiah 31:34 says, *And they shall teach no more every man his neighbour, and every man his brother, saying, Know the LORD: for they shall all know me, from the least of them unto the greatest of them, saith the LORD.* Now is the time when the people of God must intimately know the Lord, through a personal connection with Him, being guided by His Spirit, and taught by His anointing. Therefore, every true believer can be an eyewitness.

THE PROPHETIC REVOLUTION

Through Realization of Biblical Prophecies

The eyewitnesses are aware of the prophecies of Scripture and have confidence because they know the surety of biblical prophecy. They watch for the prophecies of Scripture that are yet to come.

1 Chronicles 12:32 And of the children of Issachar, which were men that had understanding of the times, to know what Israel ought to do.

They are like the children of Issachar because they are prophetically literate. Being aware of the signs of the times and sensitive to God's prophetic voice, they know what is required for the season. The eyewitnesses can be found active in God's current move upon the earth. And they are usually motivating others towards the worldwide move of God in the last days.

Luke 24:27 And beginning at Moses and all the prophets, he expounded unto them in all the scriptures the things concerning himself.

Just as the Apostles knew how Jesus fulfilled the scriptural prophecies of the Messiah, the eyewitnesses are aware of the biblical prophecies that point to the second return of Jesus Christ. Additionally, their ears are open to the Spirit of God so that they know what God is saying to the church in the last days.

Luke 2:25-30 And, behold, there was a man in Jerusalem, whose name was Simeon; and the same man was just and devout, waiting for the consolation of Israel: and the Holy Ghost was upon him. And it was revealed unto him by the Holy Ghost, that he should not see death, before he had seen the Lord's Christ. And he came by the Spirit into the temple: and when the parents brought in the child Jesus, to do for him after the custom of the law, Then took he him up in his arms, and blessed God, and said, Lord, now lettest thou thy servant depart in peace, according to thy word: For mine eyes have seen thy salvation...

Like Simeon, the eyewitnesses are looking to see the fulfillment of God's move on the earth. They look for the prophetic hand of God in the church and their own lives. Simeon was devout. He was anticipating and looking for the first coming of the Messiah. He was a man of the Spirit; the Holy Spirit was upon Him, and he followed the voice of the Lord. In the same manner, only devoutly committed Christians, who are anticipating Christ return, and listening to the Spirit will be able to see the fulfillment of prophecy in our time. They will see and walk in the movement of God's revival, and so they will be catalysts of world revival. Through prophetic insight, they will see and actuate the prophetic fulfillment of world revival.

They See in the Spirit

God speaks to them by His Spirit and even through visions and dreams. Although many of the first century Jews saw the miracles of Jesus, it was only those who heard from God that recognized he was the Messiah. Peter boldly proclaimed that Jesus was the Christ, not moved by the opinions of men because God the Father had revealed it to him. The apostle Peter opened the door of salvation to the Gentiles; however, it was only after the Lord spoke to him through a vision, and led him to the house of a Gentile. Although Jesus had told them that the gospel would be brought to the Gentiles, only through the leading of the Spirit were they able to walk into that prophetic reality. So we see that to realize and actualize prophetic fulfillment, the Holy Spirit had to give prophetic insight.

They Hear the Secrets

Just as Daniel heard from God about His secret plans for Israel, the eyewitnesses hear the secret things of God. Daniel understood by the Scriptures, the prophetic plan for the children of Israel's return from captivity in Babylon and restoration to the land of Israel. Understanding the time, Daniel began to seek God; and as a result, God spoke to him concerning Israel's immediate restoration and God's mysterious plan for the nation. The eyewitnesses begin from the foundation of biblical prophecy, seeking to do God's will as they walk in the fear of the Lord. Consequently, God shows them His secrets (Psalm 25:14).

Nebuchadnezzar, the king of Babylon, had a dream that he wanted his astrologers to interpret, but without letting them know the contents of the dream. After the failure of the wise men and astrologers of Babylon, Daniel requested the opportunity to interpret the dream. Daniel then took the time to seek God about the dream, and so God revealed to Daniel the dream and gave him the interpretation. Daniel worshipped God for revealing the secrets of the dream. Due to their devoted relationship with the Lord, the eyewitnesses hear God's secrets and receive revelations of coming events happening in the world.

Similarly, Joseph interpreted the dream of the baker and the butler while in prison in Egypt (Genesis 40). Then later, Joseph interpreted the dream of Pharaoh and provided prophetic guidance into what to do for that time (Genesis 41). It was God who revealed these secrets to Joseph. God is raising up eyewitnesses who will hear the secrets hidden from men and give insight into what God is doing. The eyewitnesses exist in the marketplaces, in government halls, in communities, in neighborhoods – children of God who hear from God concerning the things happening in our time. The eyewitnesses will be able to give prophetic insight to those around them, because they "see" the prophetic hands of God.

They are Watchmen

Since the eyewitnesses see the prophetic hands of God and have prophetic insight into current events, they are the watchmen of our time. Watchmen are like security officers. They were stationed in a high place in the land so that they could see any approaching dangers to the city or nation. If they saw an enemy or other types of threats against the land, they would then sound an alarm so that the people may be warned (Ezekiel 33). The eyewitnesses serve as watchmen; they are keeping watch in the Spirit, and sounding an alarm in their preaching.

The eyewitnesses watch for the signs of the times. They are aware of the biblical admonitions regarding the season in which Christ will return. For instance, when they see the increasing influence of the spirit of the antichrist in society, they sound an alarm through preaching. When they see the increasing elemental disasters, rumors of wars, false Christs, and false prophets, they sound the alarm.

God has his eyewitnesses strategically placed as watchmen throughout the world. Some operate in the ministry office of prophet and are sent to alert the body of Christ. Most are regular believers who are stationed in government halls, school rooms, civil organizations, marketplaces, and other societal environments; there, they sound the alarm seeing the signs of the times. Eyewitnesses are all over the world, and God has given them the prophetic insight so that they can warn those around them to escape the wrath to come. God has witnesses in the earth. He will not judge without showing His witnesses, and compelling them to warn. Once the watchmen have done their duty, every human who hears the warning to escape the judgment to come, are accountable for their actions.

You can be an eyewitness for Christ. If you are willing to devote yourself to God like Simeon in daily submission to the leading of the Spirit, then God can show you the things that will happen on the earth. You can pray: open my eyes Lord and let me see in the Spirit, and warn the world to repent for your coming is near.

14

PROPHETIC LITERACY

THE EYEWITNESSES ARE prophetically literate. What is prophetic literacy? First, prophetic literacy is having a basic understanding of biblical prophecy for knowledge of how to live and what to do in the current time. It is being aware of the general prophecies of Scripture concerning Christ in His first coming, and the signs of the times toward His second coming. Secondly, prophetic literacy is the willingness to embrace prophetic utterance and revelation by testing prophecies given, and holding on to true prophecy.

In this time, every believer needs to gain prophetic literacy. Without having a basic understanding of prophecy, a believer can become blind to prophetic dangers and pitfalls of the time. Prophetic literacy does not mean that you need to know Greek and Hebrew and be a scholar on eschatology (the study of the end times). More readily, I have known elderly saints with no seminary training, who were keenly aware of prophetic dangers and end-time signs, and willingly warned others. They became prophetically literate through their devotion to the Word of God and prayer.

THE PROPHETIC REVOLUTION

Becoming prophetically literate begins with having biblical literacy. The entire Bible is a prophetic book. You cannot understand prophecy without first committing to prayerfully reading and studying the Bible. Beginning from the first three chapters of Genesis, there are prophecies of the future both directly and metaphorically. For example, in Genesis, it emphatically states that *"for this cause shall a man leave his mother and father and cleave unto his wife"*; this was an establishment and a prophecy on the institution of marriage. Genesis also establishes that men would replenish the earth. Going further, Genesis prophesies of the suffering that men and women would face due to their sin. We also see the prophecy of the coming Redeemer, Jesus Christ. The book of Revelation concludes with a warning not to subtract nor add to the prophecies written within it. The Bible is a prophetic book. Therefore, to become prophetically literate, the believer must become a student of the Bible - reading, studying, memorizing, and meditating on it. Believers who want God to use them in this prophetic revolution must be faithful students of the Word of God both studying it and applying it in their lives.

Assuming you have committed to learning and applying the Word of God faithfully, you can immediately begin to increase your prophetic literacy. Here, I will name a few prophetic areas of the Bible that every believer should become familiar with: (1) fulfilled prophecies of Christ's first coming; (2) prophecies of Christ's return; (3) Old Testament foreshadows of worldwide judgment and salvation; (4) general prophecies of the last days before Christ's return; (5) the general themes in the book of Revelation.

Fulfilled Prophecies of Christ

The Spirit of Prophecy moved the Old Testament prophets to speak beforehand of Christ's suffering and His subsequent glory. *1 Peter 1:10-11 Of which salvation the prophets have inquired and searched diligently, who prophesied of the grace that should come unto you: Searching what, or what manner of time the Spirit of Christ which was in them did signify, when it testified beforehand the sufferings of Christ, and the glory that should follow.* The Spirit of Prophecy, who is the Spirit of Christ (Revelation 19:10) revealed before the sufferings of Christ and the subsequent effects.

Christ's virgin birth, place of birth, sufferings, burial, and resurrection were all prophesied in the Scriptures. The first century Jewish leaders, while aware of some of the prophecies of the Messiah, were blind to its understanding and fulfillment. The Bible speaks of two devout Jews who were aware that Jesus Christ was the promised Messiah. The first was Anna.

> *Luke 2:36 – 38 And there was one Anna, a prophetess, the daughter of Phanuel, of the tribe of Aser: she was of a great age, and had lived with an husband seven years from her virginity; And she was a widow of about fourscore and four years, which departed not from the temple, but served God with fastings and prayers night and day. And she coming in that instant gave thanks likewise unto the Lord, and spake of him to all them that looked for redemption in Jerusalem.*

Note that Anna the prophetess while devout in prayer and service to God diligently waited for the coming of the Messiah, and so God made her fully aware when Jesus arrived in the temple. Surely, the Bible truthfully speaks when it says in Psalm

25:14 that the *"secret of the Lord is with them that fear him."* Those who are devoted to God in prayer and service will have prophetic insight. We see that Simeon, who was also aware that Christ was the promised Messiah, had similar characteristics to Anna.

> *Luke 2:25-30 And, behold, there was a man in Jerusalem, whose name was Simeon; and the same man was just and devout, waiting for the consolation of Israel: and the Holy Ghost was upon him. And it was revealed unto him by the Holy Ghost, that he should not see death, before he had seen the Lord's Christ. And he came by the Spirit into the temple: and when the parents brought in the child Jesus, to do for him after the custom of the law, Then took he him up in his arms, and blessed God, and said, Lord, now lettest thou thy servant depart in peace, according to thy word: For mine eyes have seen thy salvation,*

Simeon was devoted to serving God and was anticipating the arrival of the coming Messiah. He was a man who was sensitive and attentive to the leading of the Spirit. He was led by the Holy Spirit to witness the arrival of the coming Messiah.

Again, to be prophetically literate, one must be a devout follower of Christ who maintains a close relationship with God in prayer and service. The worldly, shallow Christian will lack prophetic literacy and insight.

The disciples did not fully grasp the prophecies of Christ until Jesus gave the understanding after His resurrection. Jesus opened the eyes of the apostles to the prophecies concerning Christ's sufferings and resurrection. God wants us to be literate in the Old Testament prophecies of Christ. A good place to start is by knowing and memorizing the Genesis prophecy that an offspring of the woman would be the one to defeat Satan in *Genesis 3:15*. *And I will put enmity between thee and the woman, and between thy seed and her seed; it shall bruise thy head, and thou shalt bruise his heel.* This prophecy sets the stage for the coming Redeemer, Jesus Christ. Jesus Christ is the ultimate seed of the woman who bruised the serpent's head through his death on the cross and subsequent resurrection.

Instead of commenting on the Old Testament prophecies of Christ's first coming, the upcoming table lays out some of the prophecies, and the New Testament references on how they were fulfilled. Study these on your own and ask the Lord to lead you to see more of the Messianic prophecies throughout Scripture.

Fulfilled Prophecies of Christ

Topic	Old Testament Prophecy	Fulfillment
Seed of the Woman	Genesis 3:15 And I will put enmity between thee and the woman, and between thy seed and her seed; it shall bruise thy head, and thou shalt bruise his heel.	Colossians 2:15 And having spoiled principalities and powers, he made a shew of them openly, triumphing over them in it.
Virgin Birth	Isaiah 7:14 Therefore the Lord himself shall give you a sign; Behold, a virgin shall conceive, and bear a son, and shall call his name Immanuel.	Matthew 1:21-23 And she shall bring forth a son, and thou shalt call his name JESUS: for he shall save his people from their sins. Now all this was done, that it might be fulfilled which was spoken of the Lord by the prophet, saying, Behold, a virgin shall be with child, and shall bring forth a son

Birthplace	Micah 5:2 But thou, Bethlehem Ephratah, though thou be little among the thousands of Judah, yet out of thee shall he come forth unto me that is to be ruler in Israel; whose goings forth have been from of old, from everlasting.	Matthew 2:1, Now when Jesus was born in Bethlehem of Judaea

Context: Matthew 2:1-6 |
| Deity of Christ | Isaiah 9:6 For unto us a child is born, unto us a son is given: and the government shall be upon his shoulder: and his name shall be called Wonderful, Counseller, The mighty God, The everlasting Father, The Prince of Peace. | John 20:28 And Thomas answered and said unto him [Jesus], My Lord and my God |

THE PROPHETIC REVOLUTION

Forerunner	Isaiah 40:3 The voice of him that crieth in the wilderness, Prepare ye the way of the LORD, make straight in the desert a highway for our God. Also: Malachi 3:1	Matthew 3:3 For this is he that was spoken of by the prophet Esaias, saying, The voice of one crying in the wilderness, Prepare ye the way of the Lord, make his paths straight.
Bore the Sins of the World	Isaiah 53:5-6 But he was wounded for our transgressions, he was bruised for our iniquities: the chastisement of our peace was upon him; and with his stripes we are healed. 6All we like sheep have gone astray; we have turned everyone to his own way; and the LORD hath laid on him the iniquity of us all.	1 Peter 2:24 Who his own self bare our sins in his own body on the tree, that we, being dead to sins, should live unto righteousness: by whose stripes ye were healed.

Pierced	Psalm 22:16 …they pierced my hands and my feet.	John 20:27 Then saith he to Thomas, Reach hither thy finger, and behold my hands; and reach hither thy hand, and thrust it into my side: and be not faithless, but believing.
Bones not Broken	Psalm 22:17 I may tell all my bones: they look and stare upon me.	John 19:33 But when they came to Jesus, and saw that he was dead already, they brake not his legs:
Garments Gambled	Psalm 22:18 They part my garments among them, and cast lots upon my vesture.	Matthew 27:35 And they crucified him, and parted his garments, casting lots
Marred	Is 52:14 As many were astonied at thee; his visage was so marred more than any man, and his form more than the sons of men:	John 19:1 Then Pilate therefore took Jesus, and scourged him.

THE PROPHETIC REVOLUTION

Bruising & Death	Isaiah 53:5 But he was wounded for our transgressions, he was bruised for our iniquities: the chastisement of our peace was upon him; and with his stripes we are healed	John 19:1, 18 Where they crucified him, and two other with him, on either side one, and Jesus in the midst.
Resurrection	Psalm 16:10 For thou wilt not leave my soul in hell; neither wilt thou suffer thine Holy One to see corruption. Also Psalm 22:22	Matthew 28:6 He is not here: for he is risen, as he said. Come, see the place where the Lord lay Also Acts 2:27-28
Ascension	Psalm 68:18 Thou hast ascended on high, thou hast led captivity captive: thou hast received gifts for men	Acts 1:9 …while they beheld, he was taken up; and a cloud received him out of their sight. Also Luke 24:50-53; Acts 1:9-11

There are many more prophecies that were fulfilled in the Messiah, Jesus Christ, but these are sufficient to begin developing your prophetic literacy. From there, you can continue to study and explore further. Memorize about 3-5 of these Messianic prophecies and how they were fulfilled. Then become familiar with the chapters where Messianic prophecies can be found (Isaiah 9, Isaiah 53, Psalm 22, Psalm 110). Next, let us look into prophecies of Christ's second coming.

Prophecies of Christ's Return

Anna and Simeon were convinced of the prophecies of Christ's first coming causing them to pray about, look for, and live in expectation of it. Christians today need to have that same conviction and anticipation of Christ's second coming. Concerning Christ's return, the prophetically literate will anticipate it, pray about it, live for it, and preach about it. Therefore, to increase your prophetic literacy, Christians must become familiar with the prophecies of Christ's second coming. Here, I am not talking about understanding all the details of end-time studies. Sure, we must reject any doctrine that claims Christ's second coming has already passed or that denies Christ's literal return. But, the purpose in this chapter is for every believer to have the biblical conviction to prepare for and prophesy Christ's return.

The New Testament refers to Christ's return over 300 times. I will only list a few of the scriptural prophecies of Christ's second return, so that we can glean some of the major aspects of it.

And, so that we can confidently declare this ultimate biblical prophecy.

His Return is Literal

Acts 1:10-11 And when he had spoken these things, while they beheld, he was taken up; and a cloud received him out of their sight. And while they looked stedfastly toward heaven as he went up, behold, two men stood by them in white apparel. Which also said, Ye men of Galilee, why stand ye gazing up into heaven? this same Jesus, which is taken up from you into heaven, shall so come in like manner as ye have seen him go into heaven.

The return of Christ will not be invisible or merely a spiritual event. There will be a literal bodily return of Christ in the same manner in which he left.

Christ Will Gather Believers

Matthew 24:31 And he shall send his angels with a great sound of a trumpet, and they shall gather together his elect from the four winds, from one end of heaven to the other.

John 14:3 And if I go and prepare a place for you, I will come again, and receive you unto myself; that where I am, there ye may be also.

Hebrews 9:28 So Christ was once offered to bear the sins of many; and unto them that look for him shall he appear the second time without sin unto salvation.

2 Thessalonians 2:1 Now we beseech you, brethren, by the coming of our Lord Jesus Christ, and by our gathering together unto him

The Church Will Be Raptured

1 Corinthians 15:51-52 Behold, I shew you a mystery; We shall not all sleep, but we shall all be changed, In a moment, in the twinkling of an eye, at the last trump: for the trumpet shall sound, and the dead shall be raised incorruptible, and we shall be changed.

1 Thessalonians 4:16-17 For the Lord himself shall descend from heaven with a shout, with the voice of the archangel, and with the trump of God: and the dead in Christ shall rise first: Then we which are alive and remain shall be caught up together with them in the clouds, to meet the Lord in the air: and so shall we ever be with the Lord.

The term rapture means caught up. Born again believers will be caught up to meet Jesus in the air. At the rapture, our bodies will be changed to an incorruptible body.

Day and Hour Unknown

Matthew 24:36 But of that day and hour knoweth no man, no, not the angels of heaven, but my Father only.

Matthew 24:44 Therefore be ye also ready: for in such an hour as ye think not the Son of man cometh.

1 Thessalonians 5:2 For yourselves know perfectly that the day of the Lord so cometh as a thief in the night.

His Coming is Soon

Revelation 3:11 Behold, I come quickly: hold that fast which thou hast, that no man take thy crown.

Revelation 22:12 And, behold, I come quickly; and my reward is with me, to give every man according as his work shall be.

Only the Watchful Will Be Ready

Luke 21:34-36 And take heed to yourselves, lest at any time your hearts be overcharged with surfeiting, and drunkenness, and cares of this life, and so that day come upon you unawares. For as a snare shall it come on all them that dwell on the face of the whole earth. Watch ye therefore, and pray always, that ye may be accounted worthy to escape all these things that shall come to pass, and to stand before the Son of man.

The Ultimate Worldwide Climatic Event

Matthew 24:26-27 Wherefore if they shall say unto you, Behold, he is in the desert; go not forth: behold, he is in the secret chambers; believe it not. For as the lightning cometh out of the east, and shineth even unto the west; so shall also the coming of the Son of man be.

Matthew 24:30 And then shall appear the sign of the Son of man in heaven: and then shall all the tribes of the earth mourn, and they shall see the Son of man coming in the clouds of heaven with power and great glory.

Luke 21:27 And then shall they see the Son of man coming in a cloud with power and great glory.

Revelation 1:7 Behold, he cometh with clouds; and every eye shall see him, and they also which pierced him: and all kindreds of the earth shall wail because of him. Even so, Amen.

1 Thessalonians 4:16 For the Lord himself shall descend from heaven with a shout, with the voice of the archangel, and with the trump of God: and the dead in Christ shall rise first:

All Christians should be familiar with these verses on the second coming of Christ. To prophesy of Christ's return in preaching and evangelism, believers should memorize three to five (3-5) of these verses and be ready to declare them. Declaring the prophecies of Scripture increases one's prophetic conviction and insight.

Foreshadows in the Old Testament

There are events and characters in the Old Testament that foreshadow our salvation in Christ, and the future judgment coming upon the world. These Old Testament events paint a prophetic picture of the judgment to come, and the way of salvation. Having familiarity with these Old Testament foreshadows significantly increases one's comprehension of biblical prophecy, and provides prophetic insight into the current time.

The Worldwide Flood, and the Ark

Luke 17:26-27 And as it was in the days of Noe, so shall it be also in the days of the Son of man. They did eat, they drank, they married wives, they were given in marriage, until the day that Noe entered into the ark, and the flood came, and destroyed them all.

Before judgment upon the world men will indulge in eating, drinking, and marrying. Life will continue in its normal affair. It will not be apparent that time is up. Humankind will be having the time of its life.

1 Peter 3:20-21 Which sometime were disobedient, when once the longsuffering of God waited in the days of Noah, while the ark was a preparing, wherein few, that is, eight souls were saved by water. The like figure whereunto even baptism doth also now save us (not the putting away of the filth of the flesh, but the answer of a good conscience toward God,) by the resurrection of Jesus Christ:

2 Peter 2:5 And spared not the old world, but saved Noah the eighth person, a preacher of righteousness, bringing in the flood upon the world of the ungodly;

The ark represents a type of salvation. Salvation through Jesus Christ is the ark of these last days. The "Noahs" of these last days are the remnant of believers who are preaching the gospel of Christ and prophesying His soon return. These end-time "Noahs" are pointing the way into the ark so that humankind can escape the wrath of God to come upon the world.

Sodom and Gomorrah

Luke 17:28-32 Likewise also as it was in the days of Lot; they did eat, they drank, they bought, they sold, they planted, they builded; But the same day that Lot went out of Sodom it rained fire and brimstone from heaven, and destroyed them all. Even thus shall it be in the day when the Son of man is revealed. 31In that day, he which shall be upon the housetop, and his stuff in the house, let him not come down to take it away: and he that is in the field, let him likewise not return back. Remember Lot's wife.

Just before the coming judgment, the world will be in a similar state as it was in Sodom and Gomorrah. Humankind will be living life as if there is no God - indulging in the things of this world, just as they did in the days of Noah. Therefore, Christ's second coming will be sudden and without warning because of the blindness of the people on the earth. They will take their fill of pleasure in the things of the earth lacking consideration for eternal things.

2 Peter 2:6-9 And turning the cities of Sodom and Gomorrha into ashes condemned them with an overthrow, making them an ensample unto those that after should live ungodly; And delivered just Lot, vexed with the filthy conversation of the wicked: (For that righteous man dwelling among them, in seeing and hearing, vexed his righteous soul from day to day with their unlawful deeds;) The Lord knoweth how to deliver the godly out of temptations, and to reserve the unjust unto the day of judgment to be punished:

However, make no mistake; judgment is surely coming. As the cities of Sodom and Gomorrah were burned to ashes, all evil works will be burned up with extreme heat. The ungodly will burn in a fire of judgment; and like Lot, the righteous will be delivered from the wrath to come. Lot lived among the people of Sodom and Gomorrah but was grieved with their sinful behavior. Even so, believers today should not grow comfortable with the rampant increase of sin and sexual immorality. Becoming engrossed with the things of the world blinds our eyes to the prophetic reality. The heart of Lot's wife was bound to Sodom and Gomorrah, preventing her from seeing her way of escape. Prophetic insight comes only to those who keep their hearts pure from the things of the world.

Israel's Deliverance from Egypt and Walk Through the Dessert

1 Corinthians 10:6-11 Now these things were our examples, to the intent we should not lust after evil things, as they also lusted. Neither be ye idolaters, as were some of them; as it is written, The people sat down to eat and drink, and rose up to play. Neither let us commit fornication, as some of them committed, and fell in one day three and twenty thousand. Neither let us tempt Christ, as some of them also tempted, and were destroyed of serpents. Neither murmur ye, as some of them also murmured, and were destroyed of the destroyer. Now all these things happened unto them for ensamples: and they are written for our admonition, upon whom the ends of the world are come.

The events of Israel's deliverance from Egypt and their journey through the wilderness foreshadows our own walk with Christ.

The Passover Lamb is a foreshadowing of Christ who is truly our Passover Lamb. As Israel escaped death through the blood of a lamb, we have escaped death and corruption through the blood of the Lamb, Jesus Christ. Egypt represents bondage. We were in spiritual bondage in Egypt. Like how God delivered the Israelites from slavery, by God's power, we have been delivered from the spiritual bondage of Egypt. The passage through the Red Sea typifies baptism. Through the Red Sea, the Egyptian taskmasters perished, and the children of Israel walked into their new reality. Even so, baptism represents a burying of the old man, and the rising of a new man in Jesus Christ. However, failing to achieve full redemption, many of the Israelites sinned and died in the wilderness, even though they had experienced salvation from Egypt. Given all this, it is evident that Israel serves as an example of the things we should be careful of in these last days.

Israel's example of temptations and sins are written as an admonition *"upon whom the ends of the world are come"*. The record of Israel's temptations through the wilderness serves as a prophetic witness of the temptations that believers would face in the end-times. Last day believers should not be negligent in our position in Christ but should take heed, lest when we think we stand we fall.

So, we see by this prophetic example that the following temptations would be common on end-time believers:

- Lust
- Idolatry
- Sexual Immorality

> Tempting the Lord – The Israelites accused the Lord by mischaracterizing His intention for taking them out of Egypt. They were missing the pleasures of Egypt, desiring food in the wilderness, and said that God brought them out of Egypt to die in the wilderness. So they tested the Lord's character and ability.

> Murmuring – The Israelites murmured against Moses, and God. Today, some Christians enjoy murmuring and complaining about their leaders and church, instead of focusing on God's will.

General Prophecies

There are general prophetic warnings throughout the Bible that believers should know. They provide insight into the state of the world in the last days. Committed believers who are knowledgeable of these will have the scriptural tools to be aware of the signs of the times. Below is a listing of some of these general prophecies.

From Matthew 24

Answering the questions of His disciples, Jesus gives us a glimpse of the state of the world as it approaches the season of His return. He warns believers to remain watchful and faithful during the season before His return (Matthew 24:45-51). Jesus tells us in advance that there will be false prophets and Christs, and that we should not give heed to them. Some will say that Christ has returned at a certain location; Jesus insists that we should not listen since His return will be a universal event.

- False Christs and False Prophets Matthew 24:5, 11
- International Wars Matthew 24:6-7
- Multiple Worldwide Calamities Matthew 24:7
- Multiple Worldwide Earthquakes Matthew 24:7
- Worldwide Persecution Matthew 24:9
- Betrayal Matthew 24:10
- Massive Sinfulness - *Matthew 24:12 And because iniquity shall abound, the love of many shall wax cold.*
- Decrease in Loving God

1 Timothy 4:1-3

The apostle Paul tells us that the Spirit clearly speaks on the threats to Christianity that will take place in the last days.

- A Falling Away from the Faith
- Giving Heed to Seducing Spirits – Seducing spirits lure people into false doctrines using sensual desires and lusts.
- Hypocrisy and Dead Consciences – When a person's conscience is dead, they no longer acknowledge their sins, but justify themselves by unbiblical values and doctrines.
- Doctrines of Devils
    - Forbidding to Marry
    - Commanding Dietary Laws

2 Timothy 3

Here the scripture tells us that the last days will be difficult times when humankind will act out in all types of evil ways. Christians are admonished not to follow these things, and to avoid those who practice a dead religion.

- ➢ Love of Self and Money
- ➢ Self-Conceited
- ➢ Rebellious to Parents
- ➢ Ungrateful
- ➢ Cruel
- ➢ Hateful of Good Things
- ➢ Lovers of Pleasure than God
- ➢ Powerless/Dead Religion

2 Thessalonians 2:1-4 and 1 John 2:17

The apostle Paul tells the Thessalonians of certain things that will take place before the second return of Christ. The apostle Paul states that there will first be a falling away from the faith. Additionally, before Christ returns to earth, the antichrist will appear. The antichrist is described as a wicked one, who opposes God, godliness, and sets himself up as God. The apostle John tells us that the spirit of the antichrist is already at work in the world, a sign that it is the last days. If that time was already the last days, how much more are we in the last days now and should beware of the antichrist spirit that is already operating.

General Understanding of the Book of Revelation

The book of Revelation gives a special promise to those who seek to understand the book. In Revelation 1:3 the scripture states: *Blessed is he that readeth, and they that hear the words of this prophecy, and keep those things which are written therein: for the time is at hand.* Some Christians may avoid the book of Revelation because of its heavy use of apocalyptic language. However, God gives prophetic insight to those who seek to understand it. It would be incomplete to address prophetic literacy without looking at the main themes of Revelation, and how it commands us to live in the last days. The promised blessing in the book of Revelation are for those who do three (3) things: read the prophecy, hear the prophecy, and keep the commands of the book. Growing in prophetic literacy then demands that we read the prophecies of Revelation, listen to preaching and teaching concerning it, and keep the commands of the book.

When we read and study the book of Revelation, certain themes stand out. The following only gives a summary overview of some of the main themes

- ➢ The Glory of the Resurrected Christ (Revelation 1:5-8; 11, 13-18; 5:5-14; 19:11-16).

- ➢ The Certain Coming of Christ as a Universal Event (Revelation 1:7; 14:14;).

- ➢ Worldwide Deception through Satan, the Antichrist, and the False Prophet (Revelation 12:9; 13; 16:14; 17:7-18; 20:7-10).

➤ The Perseverance and Victory of God's People (Revelation 6:9; 7:3, 14; 12:11; 15:2; 20:4, 6;

➤ God's Ultimate Victory over Satan and his Works (Revelation 19:17-21; 20:2-3; 20:10).

➤ Certain Judgment on Evil, the World, and the Devil (Revelation 6, 8, - Seven Seals and Seven Trumpets; 15-16 - Seven Vials; 17-18 - Babylon's Destruction; 19:20; 20:10 – Final Judgment on the Antichrist, False Prophet, and Satan).

➤ Rewards for the Faithful (Revelation 2:7, 11, 17, 26; 3:4-5, 11-12; 21; 17:14).

➤ The Coming New Heavens and New Earth (Revelation 21 -22).

The book of Revelation shows that to have the correct prophetic perspective, we must fully appreciate the glory of the resurrected Christ, the one who died for us and redeemed us out of sin. Christ will be returning in full glory, and every eye shall see Him. The prophetically literate understand that deception continues to rise around the world, and the spirit of the antichrist is at work. Amid this, those who remain faithful will receive rewards from God. But the devil, his agents, and works will ultimately be defeated once and for all. All will be judged. Finally, all things will be made new. Without having the prophetic perspective outlined in the book of Revelation, the believer will lack the prophetic insight to live victoriously in the present world.

Revelation 1:3 pronounces blessings on those who read, hear, and keep the commands of Revelation. We receive the blessedness of prophetic insight when we keep the commandments written in Revelation. What are the commandments given to us in the book of Revelation? The commandments in Revelation that we should keep are not often emphasized. God gives explicit instructions to His people and specific instructions to the churches. The upcoming table lists these things.

Commands of the Book of Revelation

Command	Verses	Notes
Hear what the Spirit Says to the Churches.	2:7, 11, 17, 29; 3:6, 13, 22	Listening and being sensitive to the Spirit is an essential characteristic of Prophetic literacy.
Remember your first state, repent, and do the first works.	2:5; 3:3.	Victors of prophecy maintain the vigor of the faith with the burning passion of their first love.
Do not fear satan's attacks.	2:10	Expect persecutions, trials, and betrayals, but do not be afraid.
Be faithful unto death.	2:10; 22:6	The faithful will gain rewards.

THE PROPHETIC REVOLUTION

Repent of allowing false doctrine.	2:14; 2:20-24	God condemns doctrines that give a license to sexual immorality and idolatry. He calls for repentance of even tolerating these things. Tolerating false doctrines blinds the eye to the prophetic reality.
Hold fast to truth.	2:25; 3:3, 11	Those with prophetic insight will zealously embrace to truth of the faith.
Be watchful.	3:2; 16:15	It's necessary to be watchful to recognize prophetic warning and fulfillments.
Be zealous and repent.	3:19	Lukewarm "Christians" are blind to the prophetic reality. God calls us to be zealous in our dedication to Him, and repent of lukewarmness.
Come out of Babylon.	18:4	Without getting into the specific symbolism of Babylon, we know at the general level it represents worldliness. We are commanded to be separate from the world, lest we partake in their judgment.

Rejoice in expectation of the marriage supper of the Lamb.	19:7	Christians must live in anticipation of meeting the Lamb of God. Keeping this hope firmly alive ignites purity continually.
Proclaim "come".	22:17	A mark of the prophetically literate church is that they will be calling the world to "Come".
Maintain the sanctity of the Scriptures.	22:18-19	Honestly maintaining the truth written in the Bible is a prerequisite for prophetic insight. The one who takes away or adds to Scripture has already despised and thrown away the Spirit of Prophecy. Sadly, in fulfillment of prophecy, some are already breaking this command by creating Bibles that subtract commands against homosexuality, assigning feminine pronouns to God, and undermining the Deity of Christ

THE PROPHETIC REVOLUTION

As it is the final prophetic unveiling in the Bible, believers should give heed to the commands written in it, and understand its general themes. Prophetic literacy will not be gained only by theological knowledge and scriptural memorization, but by living in the light of Scripture. The believer who knows and keeps the commands of prophetic scripture are ready to see through the eyes of God.

Godly believers who are aware of the general biblical prophecies, anticipate the Lord's return, and remain consistent in prayer, will have spiritual discernment. Shallow living Christians, who ignore the urgency of the time, and get engrossed in the pleasures of the world will be blind to the signs of the times. The devout and committed believer who expects Christ's soon return will have the insight to see and embrace the revelations and utterances that are from the throne of God.

15

THE LAST STANDOFF

> *1 Kings 19:15-18 And the LORD said unto him, Go, return on thy way to the wilderness of Damascus: and when thou comest, anoint Hazael to be king over Syria: And Jehu the son of Nimshi shalt thou anoint to be king over Israel: and Elisha the son of Shaphat of Abelmeholah shalt thou anoint to be prophet in thy room. And it shall come to pass, that him that escapeth the sword of Hazael shall Jehu slay: and him that escapeth from the sword of Jehu shall Elisha slay. Yet I have left me seven thousand in Israel, all the knees which have not bowed unto Baal, and every mouth which hath not kissed him.*

WE ARE NOW in the time of the last standoff. The commission to the church to spread the gospel of Jesus Christ to every part of the globe is still unfinished. The work needs to be done, but it cannot be completed by a selected few spiritual leaders. It requires a prophetic revolution.

After a mighty accomplishment, Elijah was discouraged, but there was still work to be done. Elijah prophesied of famine upon the land in a time when the people of Israel forsook God, and Jezebel killed the prophets. There was a paramount showdown between Elijah and the false prophets of Baal, as

THE PROPHETIC REVOLUTION

God told Elijah to make an appearance and then He will send rain. Elijah challenged the prophets of Baal to see which God would answer by fire when called upon - the God of Israel or Baal. The false prophets of Baal were exposed as there was no answer from their gods though they cried and wounded themselves. With water surrounding the altar of God, Elijah called upon the God of Israel, and fire came down from heaven burning all on the altar. The people recognized and acknowledged that the God of Israel was the true God. They gathered the false prophets, and Elijah slaughtered them. It seems that a revival was on the way. Israel had just recommitted to acknowledging the God of Israel as the only true God. Many of the false prophets of Baal were just eliminated. However, Jezebel was still on the loose and threatened to kill Elijah. Elijah ran and hid. When God confronted Elijah, he stated that Israel had forsaken God, the prophets killed, he alone was left, and Jezebel was seeking to kill him. But the work was not done. God told him to anoint three, and then God told him that there are seven thousand (7000) that He has reserved. The reserved seven thousand is a type of the remnant remaining for a prophetic revolution.

To finish the work, God would use Elijah to appoint three to continue the work that he began, in eliminating the false prophets and their followers in Israel. But beyond those whom the prophet could anoint, God had 7000, who had not bowed. The last standoff would not only include the specially chosen but 7000 whom God had preserved.

God would have Elijah pass on the mantle for the prophetic office to Elisha. He would anoint Hazael with a political charge.

Jehu was tasked with finishing off Jezebel, and the house of Ahab. The remaining seven thousand were those who God had preserved himself, who kept His word of truth. These may not have been known by name, but they were a remnant that remained in truth.

The dramatic story of Elijah parallels what is happening in the body of Christ today. Significant work has been accomplished through the Pentecostal and Charismatic movements. Mighty healing ministries, massive evangelistic crusades, and moving conferences have impacted the church and the world.

The church must be grateful for the great men and women whom God has used. However, some are no longer with us. Some have lost credibility weakened by errors in doctrine, and laps in morality. Some portions of the church have gone a bit shy about the Pentecostal fire. Others have assimilated to the culture of tolerance and political correctness. Many of the known leaders who are still standing have grown weary of the fight from the Jezebel stronghold. But God is speaking to the church with a still small voice that He has preserved an unknown remnant to finish the work. This remnant is among the hidden because they are the regular believers of the body of Christ who have been pursuing revival.

The last standoff will take place between the unknown lay prophets and the agents of satan. The unknown lay prophets will have an unyielding devotion to Christ, and His Word, and they will prophesy with power and conviction. They will be as prophesied by the late David Wilkerson:

Suffering persecution and aware of the signs of the times, an army of true Jesus followers will continue to arise like commandos. They will be a part of an underground church that will be found preaching the return of Christ and the end of the age! They will be like a thorn in the side of the harlot church, and they will sting and sear the consciences of men by their devotion and spiritual power. Devil worshippers will be in open conflict with all these true Jesus followers.[xvii]

The Drama Unfolds

When you look at how God uses the remnant throughout Scripture, we see the character of the remnants and the drama of the standoff. The remnants are believers who walk the narrow path and have forsaken the broad ways of the world. They are like Enoch, Noah, and Lot. The drama echoes the showdown between Elijah and the prophets of Israel. Let us further describe the remnants and the standoff.

The remnants are like "Enochs" who walk with God. They have a testimony of commitment to God that captures their hearts and minds away from this world. Their unquenching faith in an increasingly God-hating world counts them ready for the world to come. The remnants hold to Paul's statement that for them to *live is Christ, and to die is gain* knowing that *to be absent from the body is to be present with the Lord.* Therefore, they live so that whether present or absent from the body they are pleasing to God. These are believers who seek to be free in their conscience before God and man. As Elijah, who was raptured away like Enoch, belonging to the world to come, the remnant will have conflict with the children of this world.

Elijah battled Jezebel and the false prophets. Jezebel was an idol worshipper and pushed her idolatrous agenda through her weak husband Ahab, King of Israel. The stronghold of Jezebel still operates today with false doctrine that promotes sexual immorality, and spiritual idolatry. Elijah was in constant conflict with Ahab, the King of Israel who allowed Jezebel to advance her evil agenda. Today, some church leaders give place to the Jezebel agenda allowing teachings that promote sexual immorality and spiritual idolatry. Some mainline churches are already "affirming" homosexual relationships and teaching a doctrine that gives license to the act. The hyper-grace doctrine is deceiving many purporting the idea that believers do not need to confess their sins, nor strive to be holy.

Believers who are committed to the truth will be in open conflict against the Jezebel stronghold in this world, and churchgoers who have bowed to it. But like Elijah, the remnant will speak with prophetic power, pray with fiery results, and move in the Spirit like the wind. Church going agents of the Jezebel stronghold will be troubled by their words and power. The preaching and prophetic power of the remnants will demolish the teachings of Jezebel and her followers, and they will respond with physical intimidation and violence. But God will reserve his remnant until there is world revival.

The final standoff will be between the "Noahs" who move in obedience to God's voice, and the mockers who do not know God. The remnant are people of faith that listen to the voice of God. They understand like Noah what they should be doing in the current time. They are not moved by the media, current trends, and the norm of everyday life. With the things of the world continuing as it is day after day, many ignore the call to come into the ark of salvation. They see no coming judgment and are blind to the signs of Christ's second coming. But the remnants are moving with urgency obeying the voice of God, preparing for a new heaven and a new earth. These "Noahs" warn others of the urgency of doing God's will. However, many mock them seeing their actions as foolish. The tension is for believers to maintain resolute obedience and faithful proclamation of truth in the face of a world that mocks their radical stand.

The final standoff will be between the righteous who are vexed by the perversion in society and the aggressive mob of sexual activists. Living in Sodom and Gomorrah, Lot's soul was vexed with the perversion in society. He tried to hold back the men of Sodom from attempting to rape the angels who came with a message of escape from judgment. The sex-crazed mob sought to break through to engage in their sexual deeds. Similarly, the current standoff is between godly believers who stand against the sexual agenda plaguing the society, and perverted sexual activists pushing for the church to embrace their agenda. In the western world, the same-sex agenda began with the promotion of marriage equality but has now extended to criminalizing preachers who speak biblical truth about same-sex relationships and gender identity. Some western countries have already enforced hate speech laws prohibiting preachers from calling same-sex relationships a sin. The drama of the final standoff is already afoot. Believers must have their ears open to the voice of the Spirit with readiness to speak and move according to God's will.

The remnant will only stand by keeping their heart free from the pleasures of the world and escaping the corruption through the leading of the Spirit. Like Lot, the remnant will have to let go of friends and relatives who love this world more than the love of God. There is no neutral ground in this end-time spiritual showdown.

The final standoff will be between those who have an ever-increasing relationship with God, and bitter "Judases" who will betray them for a piece of silver. Knowing God, the remnants will do great works proclaiming the gospel around the world, winning souls in every tribe, and compelling believers to do the work of God. Demonized through their lusts, and bowing to worldly pressure, unstable Christians will betray the remnant by aligning with political parties, securing material well-being, and protecting earthly prestige. Of course, the remnant will shine brighter and brighter, and many betrayers will miss their opportunity to repent.

The final standoff will be between those who speak the irresistible truth through the unction of the Spirit, and the heathen's rage against the Spirit's convicting power. The spirit of the antichrist is stirring the rage of the heathen against Christ and his people. Already happening in different parts of the world, increasingly believers will be threatened, persecuted, and even killed for their faith. Radical Islamists, anti-Christian governments, sociocultural elites, and lukewarm Christians will pine after ways to intimidate and silence the remnant believers. During this, Spirit-filled believers will gain a tongue that their adversaries will not be able to resist. Thus, their words will pierce the consciences of men spurring a response of repentance or disdain. Unable to resist with reason, the rebellious will rage at the remnant with mockery and contempt. But the believers will speak with uncanny boldness and wisdom that the only response their adversaries will find useful is the throwing of stones. Fixed with eyes on their Master, Jesus Christ, the remnant will remain filled with the Spirit and unmoved from their calling. They will stay fixed on the call to complete the great commission.

The last standoff is the culmination of the rising tide of the prophetic revolution. Men, women, young and old are arising to speak with prophetic power; fameless but worldwide in number, their stand will be revolutionary, shaking the strongholds and sweeping the earth with revival. Now is the time for you to be a part of it!

Appendix

Did the Prophetic Gift Cease? A Biblical Response to the Objection of Cessationism

Some teach the doctrine of cessationism that some spiritual gifts ceased after the first century or the death of the original apostles. Among cessationists, the gift of prophecy is often listed as one of the gifts that have ceased. Here, I provide a biblical rebuttal to this teaching. Most who teach the doctrine of cessationism fail to provide plain, literal scriptural evidence. Instead, they often have conjectures and assumptions from a few scriptures that do not state their claim.

Here is what the Bible plainly states regarding the continuation of spiritual gifts..

Acts 2:15-17 For these are not drunken, as ye suppose, seeing it is but the third hour of the day. But this is that which was spoken by the prophet Joel; And it shall come to pass in the last days, saith God, I will pour out of my Spirit upon all flesh: and your sons and your daughters shall prophesy, and your young men shall see visions, and your old men shall dream dreams: And on my servants and on my handmaidens I will pour out in those days of my Spirit; and they shall prophesy:

Peter gave this scripture to explain the phenomenon on the day of Pentecost when the upper room believers all spoke in tongues. Peter associated the manifestation with Joel's prophecy of the pouring out of the Spirit upon all people causing them to prophesy and receive revelations. Peter restating Joel's prophecy says, *"it shall come to pass in the last days."* If Peter's time is the last days, surely it is more so the last days today, and the manifestation of these spiritual gifts would continue. On a whole, the Bible demonstrates that the manifestation of the gift of prophecy would increase as we draw nearer to the end of time.

Acts 2:38-39 Then Peter said unto them, Repent, and be baptized every one of you in the name of Jesus Christ for the remission of sins, and ye shall receive the gift of the Holy Ghost. For the promise is unto you, and to your children, and to all that are afar off, even as many as the Lord our God shall call.

Peter said to the audience that the "promise" was unto their children, and as many as the Lord will call. The promise he is speaking of is the gift of the Holy Spirit. The audience was seeing the results of the gift as the apostles spoke in tongues.

I Corinthians 1:4-6 I thank my God always on your behalf, for the grace of God which is given you by Jesus Christ; That in every thing ye are enriched by him, in all utterance, and in all knowledge; Even as the testimony of Christ was confirmed in you: So that ye come behind in no gift; waiting for the coming of our Lord Jesus Christ

Paul was thankful to God for the gifts that were abounding in the Corinthian church. He then said that they should lack no gift as they wait for the coming of the Lord. Since the Lord has not yet come, we expect the church should continue in all the gifts. Paul corrected the Corinth church on spiritual gifts (I Corinthians 14). Therefore, Paul could have informed them that

Appendix: Did the Prophetic Gift Cease?

the gifts would cease; instead, Paul clearly states that the gifts should continue.

I Corinthians 13:9-12 For we know in part, and we prophesy in part. But when that which is perfect is come, then that which is in part shall be done away. When I was a child, I spake as a child, I understood as a child, I thought as a child: but when I became a man, I put away childish things. For now we see through a glass, darkly; but then face to face: now I know in part; but then shall I know even as also I am known.

Traditionally, cessationists used this passage in I Corinthians 13 to support their doctrine. Many have today backed away from using this scripture. A few still teach that the canon of Scripture, the completion of the Bible, is the "perfect" thing that came, so we no longer need prophecy. However, that interpretation does not fit the plain and literal sense of the text.

Rather the text is saying the following. Through the gift of prophecy we only know in part. When the "perfect" comes, we will no longer need spiritual gifts. The perfect comes when Jesus Christ returns. At that perfect time, we will see face to face, and we will know even as we are known. We have the full canon of Scripture, the Bible, but we do not see face to face, and believers do not have complete knowledge today. We will only have full knowledge and see face to face when Christ returns. Therefore, the gift of prophecy should continue until the return of Christ.

John 14:12 Verily, verily, I say unto you, He that believeth on me, the works that I do shall he do also; and greater works than these shall he do; because I go unto my Father.

Plainly, Jesus states that those who believe in him will do the works that he did and greater. The works Jesus did include miraculous manifestations. Therefore, we should expect supernatural manifestations in the church today.

Mark 16:17-18 And these signs shall follow them that believe; In my name shall they cast out devils; they shall speak with new tongues; They shall take up serpents; and if they drink any deadly thing, it shall not hurt them; they shall lay hands on the sick, and they shall recover.

The signs which include speaking in tongues would follow them that believe. This scripture did not limit the signs to the first-century believers, but to those who believe.

Ephesians 4:11-13 And he gave some, apostles; and some, prophets; and some, evangelists; and some, pastors and teachers; For the perfecting of the saints, for the work of the ministry, for the edifying of the body of Christ: Till we all come in the unity of the faith, and of the knowledge of the Son of God, unto a perfect man unto the measure of the stature of the fullness of Christ.

God gave ministry gifts, including prophets, for the equipping of the saints to do the work of ministry. It will continue until the body of Christ comes into the full stature of the fullness of Christ. All can agree that the perfecting of the body is still needed; therefore, the ministry office of the prophet is still required.

Explicit Commands

Without any need to add or take away from it, the above scriptures plainly state the continuation of the gifts until Christ's second coming. However, there are also explicit commands of Scripture that for us to obey it would necessitate the continuation of the gifts.

Appendix: Did the Prophetic Gift Cease?

I Corinthians 12:31 But covet earnestly the best gifts.

I Corinthians 14:1 Follow after charity, and desire spiritual gifts, but rather that ye may prophesy.

In the above two verses, Paul commands us to desire spiritual gifts. He makes no mention that certain gifts would cease. Furthermore, Paul emphasizes for us to seek for the gift of prophecy. There is nothing in Scripture to suggest that these instructions are not for the church today. Rather, these scriptures are given for the church to follow.

I Corinthians 14:39 Wherefore, brethren, covet to prophesy, and forbid not to speak with tongues.

Here Paul gives explicit instructions to desire to prophesy, and not to forbid speaking in tongues. When cessationists forbid tongue-speaking and prophecy, they are violating this scriptural instruction.

I Peter 4:10 As every man hath received the gift, even so minister the same one to another, as good stewards of the manifold grace of God.

Romans 12:6 Having then gifts differing according to the grace that is given to us, whether prophecy, let us prophesy according to the proportion of faith.

The above two verses compel us to operate in the gifts that we have been given. Neither of the scriptures speaks of any gift ceasing, and the New Testament never states that any of the gifts would cease before Christ's second return. The scriptures are telling us to operate in the spiritual gifts that have been given to us. Furthermore, Romans 12:6 specifically tells us that those with the gift of prophecy should prophesy. Paul, the writer of Romans and Corinthians, tells us that all believers can prophesy

(I Corinthians 14:5, 24, 31). Surely, Paul is speaking of the same gift of prophecy and telling us to operate in it by grace.

Supporting the above biblical reasons is the fact that the manifestations of spiritual gifts is taking place in the body of Christ across the world. Many prophecies of future events are being given today that consistently come to pass. Churches and ministries around the world are prophesying with accurate fulfillments. Some of them can be clearly seen at Youtube.com/harvestarmy.

Notes

1. ⁱⁱCBNNews. *2 Islamic Groups Target Nigerian Christians.* Posted: March 20, 2019. Retrieved: September 7, 2019.

   https://www1.cbn.com/cbnnews/cwn/2019/march/2-islamic-groups-target-nigerian-christians-300-killed-while-72-others-supernaturally-saved-from-firing-squad.

   Also See Open Doors. *Kenya.* Retrieved: September 7, 2019. https://www.opendoorsusa.org/christian-persecution/world-watch-list/kenya/.

2. ⁱⁱ Open Doors. *5 Things to Know About China's Big Jump on the 2019 World Watch List.* Posted: January 22, 2019. Retrieved: September 7, 2019.

   https://www.opendoorsusa.org/christian-persecution/stories/5-things-to-know-about-chinas-big-jump-on-the-2019-world-watch-list/.

3. ⁱⁱⁱ Center for Religious Liberty. *Apostasy, Blasphemy and Anti-Conversion Laws.* Retrieved: September 7, 2019.

   https://downloads.frc.org/EF/EF19D40.pdf.

4. ⁱᵛ Billy Graham Evangelistic Association. Posted: July 28, 2016. Retrieved: September 7, 2019. https://billygraham.org/decision-magazine/july-august-2016/in-europe-and-canada-hate-speech-laws-threaten-gospel-proclamation/.

5. ᵛ Pentecostals believe that speaking in tongues is the initial evidence of the baptism of the Holy Spirit. In this testimony, Pastor Guerline Reid seemed to have prophesied before speaking in tongues. However, prophesying first does not diminish the need for speaking in tongues as an initial evidence. Prophesying accompanied speaking in tongues when a set of believers in Ephesus were first baptized in the Spirit (Acts 19:6).

6. ᵛⁱ BibleHub.com. HELPS Word-Studies. *4395 Prophēteúō.* Retrieved: September 7, 2019.

   https://biblehub.com/str/greek/4395.htm.

7. ᵛⁱⁱ Rastafarianism is a religious movement largely in the island of Jamaica. Rastafarians believe that Haile Selassie I, originally named Tafari Makonnen, the emperor of Ethiopia from 1930 to 1974, is God or the return of the Messiah, Jesus Christ.

   https://www.britannica.com/biography/Haile-Selassie-I.

   They believe that Africa is the promise land for black people.

8. [viii] Jesus Culture Music comes out of the Jesus Culture Movement. Jesus Culture Church now operates in Sacramento, California. Jesusculture.com. A Google search will show many results about the ministry.

9. [ix] CD Baby. *Harvest Army Church International.* On Cd Baby, the song is described as a revelation from the Lord. Retrieved: August 23, 2019.

    https://store.cdbaby.com/cd/harvestarmysingers. See also

    https://www.youtube.com/watch?v=IPVhr8IpZPw.

10. [x] Harvest Army World Revival Facebook Page. Posted: April 9, 2019. Retrieved: August 23, 2019.

    https://www.facebook.com/HarvestArmy/posts/10161587890585273.

11. [xi] Consult the book *Pearls of Prophecy* by Bishop K. D. Collins for basic guidance on interpreting prophetic symbols.

12. [xii] Harvest Army World Revival website. Posted: December 31, 2009. Retrieved: August 15, 2019.

    http://www.harvestarmy.org/prophecy/buildings-seen-being-torn-down-certain-town-or-city.

13. [xiii] Harvest Army World Revival website. Posted: March 9, 2010. Retrieved: August 15, 2019.

    http://www.harvestarmy.org/prophecy/storms-loom-upon-east-usa.

14. [xiv] Harvest Army World Revival website. Posted: March 9, 2010. Retrieved: August 15, 2019.

    http://www.harvestarmy.org/fulfillment/earthquake-west-chile-moves-city-10-feet.

15. [xv] New York Times. *Gunman kills at Least 26 in Rural Texas Church.* Posted: November 5, 2017. Retrieved: August 14, 2019.

    https://www.nytimes.com/2017/11/05/us/church-shooting-texas.html.

16. [xvi] CBNNews. *Atlanta Church Hires Psychic Medium to Minister to Congregation.* Posted: May 27, 2019. Retrieved: August 11, 2019.

    https://www1.cbn.com/cbnnews/us/2019/may/atlanta-church-hires-psychic-medium-to-minister-to-congregation.

17. [xvii] Wilkerson, David. *The Vision and Beyond.* (Lindale, Texas: World Challenge Publication, 2003). *53.*

HARVESTERS ONLINE PUBLISHING

Harvesters Online Publishing is a Christian publishing ministry that produces and distributes content to stir revival. Our goal is to be a production and distribution center for Christian content, developing and equipping believers to be catalysts for world revival, so that they can achieve their maximum potential in Jesus Christ. We produce books, articles, podcasts, videos, and maintain a high-quality presence online for the production, promotion, and distribution of revival-stirring Christian content. For more information visit our website at www.harvestersonline.com.

Other Books:

No More Whacky Worship. No More Whacky Worship is a no-nonsense admonition of current and prevalent behavior among many named Christians – behavior that nullifies our claim to true worship. The book addresses how to identify and overcome personal and corporate practices that disqualify us from true worship. True worshippers genuinely embrace both private and corporate worship.

Creating Unbreakable Bonds Marital Intimacy on Three Levels. Discover how to build spiritual, emotional, and physical intimacy in your marriage. This book shows how to prepare for marriage, build the bonds of intimacy in marriage, and restore areas of broken intimacy in marriage. Successful marriages of the 21st century are those that are bonded on three levels - spiritually, emotionally, and physically.

In-House Blessings: The Benefits of Regular Church Attendance. This book gives a brief but comprehensive overview of the blessings of regular church attendance, and addresses common twenty-first century objections and misconceptions to faithfully attending a local church.

Grace for Single Parenting: A Spiritual Guide for Mothers Raising Godly Children. Having experienced God's grace to raise her son as a single mother, Guerline Reid presents biblical principles for single parenting. With steps for single mothers to overcome their spiritual struggles, and lead their household to victory single parents will discover that their children are channels of hope for the future, and instruments of deliverance in their current situation.

ABOUT THE AUTHOR

For over twenty years, Omaudi Reid has been active in Christian ministry as an itinerate preacher, pastor, teacher, and author. He is primarily known as a prolific Bible teacher, revival-stirring preacher, and disciple-maker, who has equipped believers to become church planters, pastors, and other church leaders. He is currently the senior pastor of the Harvest Army World Revival Arena in New York City, where he serves with passion. He endeavors to preach the gospel and stir revival in any medium possible to ignite world revival.

Bishop Omaudi Reid is the host of the weekly podcast, Arrows of Revival, with teachings and discussions that stir and shape believers to be used as instruments for God's Revival. He is the author of Creating Unbreakable Bonds: Marital Intimacy on Three Levels, No More Whacky Worship, In-House Blessings:

The Benefits of Regular Church Attendance, and The Prophetic Revolution. Many of his articles on Christian living and marriage can be found on online Christian media outlets.

A leader in mobilizing the body of Christ to fulfill the Great Commission, Bishop Reid serves as the Chairman for Worldwide Vision Day, a movement involving ministries and churches worldwide. Worldwide Vision Day occurs on the first Saturday of every quarter when believers across cultures and denominations unitedly preach the gospel in their locality on the same day. Additionally, he has been a pivotal part of spreading the vision for world revival as an executive leader in the Harvest Army Church International.

He has been married to Guerline Reid for over twenty years with three children. He has earned a Bachelor in Biblical Studies and Leadership, and a Master of Education. He has a Certificate of Advanced Graduate Study in Christian Education from Regent University. His passionate zeal for God has positively affected many across the world to rise to their God-given potential. He continues to allow God to use him as an instrument of revival to stir, equip, and release believers for ministry worldwide.

Harvesters Online Publishing
www.harvestersonline.com

www.ingramcontent.com/pod-product-compliance
Lightning Source LLC
Chambersburg PA
CBHW020406080526
44584CB00014B/1196